A publication of the
National Wildfire Coordinating Group

National Incident
Management System

Basic Land Navigation

PMS 475

MAY 2016

NFES 002865

Basic Land Navigation

May 2016
PMS 475
NFES 002865

Sponsored for National Wildfire Coordinating Group (NWCG) publication by the NWCG Operations and Training Committee. Questions regarding the content of this product should be directed to the Operations and Training Committee members listed at: https://www.nwcg.gov/committees/operations-and-training-committee/roster. Questions and comments may also be emailed to BLM_FA_NWCG_Products@blm.gov.

This publication is available electronically at: https://www.nwcg.gov. Printed copies may be ordered from the Great Basin Cache, National Interagency Fire Center, Boise, ID. For ordering procedures and costs, please refer to the annual *NFES Catalog Part 2: Publications* posted at https://www.nwcg.gov/publications/475.

Previous editions: 2007.

PREFACE

Basic Land Navigation is pre-course work for several courses in the National Wildfire Coordinating Group (NWCG) wildland fire curriculum. It is primarily designed for students to complete in a non- classroom environment; however, it is often used as a student workbook for navigation courses.

The 2007 version was developed by an interagency group of experts with direction and guidance from the Training and Development Program under authority of the NWCG. Minor revisions were made to this 2016 version.

NWCG appreciates the efforts of all those who have contributed to the development of this training product.

This page intentionally left blank

CONTENTS

INTRODUCTION

Navigating with a compass and map is an essential skill for many incident positions. Even with new technology, such as Global Positioning System (GPS) receivers, map and compass skills are still needed. Confidence with navigation skills comes with practice and proficiency. This confidence level often impacts how a person performs during a crisis – which can result in life or death decisions.

Basic Land Navigation is an introduction to land navigation. It begins with a general overview of maps. Then it specifically addresses how to read topographic maps. Next it covers various types of geographic location systems, such as latitude/longitude and Universal Transverse Mercator (UTM). This is followed by basic instructions on using a compass and clinometer. Then a general overview of the Global Positioning System is presented. The last chapter builds on skills learned in the previous chapters and adds new skills for navigation and field mapping. The three appendixes – glossary, answers to exercise, and tools/resources – include additional information as a reference.

Each chapter starts with a bulleted list of what you will learn. This is followed by a general overview of the chapter and how the information can be used. The technical content is then presented with several illustrations to facilitate understanding the concepts. Each chapter ends with the section "Checking Your Understanding," which consists of several questions. The answers to those questions are in Appendix B. Map scales may have changed during the printing of this publication; this may cause the correct answers to be slightly different than the given answers.

As you read through the chapters it will be helpful to have a U.S. Geological Survey (USGS) color topographic map to use as a reference. To complete the exercises you will need the following materials:

- Compass with adjustment for magnetic declination

- Clinometer

- Calculator

- Engineer's ruler (see Appendix C)

- Protractor (see Appendix C)

- Dot grid (see Appendix C)

- UTM grid reader (see Appendix C)

This page intentionally left blank.

Chapter 1 – OVERVIEW OF MAPS

In this chapter you will learn about:

➢ Key points when working with maps
➢ General types of maps
➢ Incident specific maps
➢ Map legend and symbols
➢ Map sources

A map is a navigational aid that represents a specific area, such as part of the earth's surface. Conventional symbols are used to identify objects and features on a map. Maps are critical communication tools for incident planning and operations, and are used for a variety of purposes, for example:

- To assist with navigation.

- To determine the location of a specific point or area (e.g., water sources, threatened resources).

- To calculate distance.

- To determine size of an area.

- To determine terrain and vegetative cover.

- To determine routes of travel.

- To determine names of streets, rivers, mountains, and other features.

- To visualize a specific area.

This chapter starts with some key points about maps. Then it discusses types of maps and incident specific maps. Additional information is provided on map legends and symbols. Finally, it describes different places to obtain maps.

Key Points When Working With Maps

When working with maps there are some key points to remember, especially when using the map in conjunction with a compass and Global Positioning System (GPS) receiver.

Datum

Most maps are made based on a datum (horizontal and vertical), which is the origin or reference point from which all points on a map are measured. Several different datums have been used to develop maps; however, commonly used datum includes: North American Datum of 1927 (NAD27), North American Datum of 1983 (NAD83), and the World Geodetic System of 1984 (WGS84).

The datum is important for Geographic Information Systems (GIS) and GPS applications to ensure consistency of map data. When using a GPS receiver the datum must be set to match the horizontal datum on the map. If the datum does not match there will be errors when plotting data on a map.

Geographic North

Maps are usually based on the geographic North Pole (geographic north or true north). This is important to remember because a compass is based on magnetic north, which is different than geographic north. Magnetic north changes over time, while geographic north does not change over time. When using a compass and map together an adjustment has to be made to the compass to account for this difference. The difference is referred to as the magnetic declination, which is discussed in Chapter 4, Using a Compass and Clinometer.

Maps Are Not Perfect

For a map to be considered reliable and accurate, a point or symbol marked on a map must be in proper relation to known landmarks or positions located on the ground. In 1947, the "United States National Map Accuracy Standards" were established as the standards of accuracy for published maps and are currently in effect. The standards require a stringent percent of accuracy within centimeters of both location and elevation points tested. However, even with these standards, maps are not absolutely accurate because:

- Maps represent a curved and uneven surface that is drawn on a flat piece of paper, which results in a distorted picture.

- There is a margin of error (human error and inadequate survey procedures) in surveys that were used to create maps. Also, there are factual matters (errors such as names, symbols of features, and the classifications of roads or woodlands); sometimes the information is wrong and names and features change.

- On incidents, if a map has been photocopied, it most likely is not to scale. It is important to watch out for this and learn how to make adjustments.

Maps Can Be Outdated

Maps are outdated from the day they are made, including USGS topographic maps (for example, new roads may not be on a map). When working on an incident try to obtain the most up-to-date map.

USGS topographic maps have the revision date in the margin.

General Types of Maps

This section discusses general types of maps: planimetric, topographic, and orthophoto.

Planimetric Maps

Planimetric maps show the positions of features without showing their relationship to the hills and valleys of the land. Examples of features on planimetric maps include rivers, lakes, roads, and boundaries.

Planimetric maps include:

- Common road maps – road atlas and city maps (Figure 1-1).

- Specific area maps – preplan maps, floor plan maps, storm drain maps, sewer and water system maps.

- Schematic maps – agency maps and aviation maps.

Figure 1-1. City map.

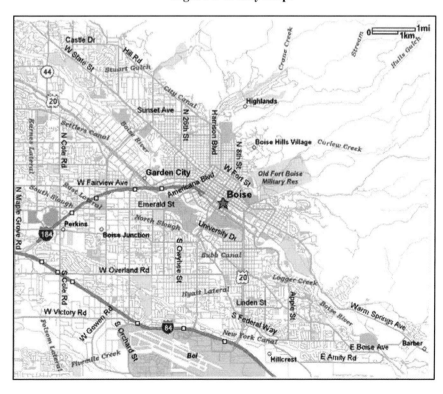

Topographic Maps

Topographic maps are different from planimetric maps because they show both the horizontal and vertical (relief) positions of features. The datum used for most currently available USGS 7.5 minute series topographical maps is the NAD27. A new datum, NAD83, is now being used and others are being developed. Most of the topographic maps used on incidents are produced by the USGS or USDA Forest Service. These maps are often used as the base map to develop incident specific maps, such as the Situation Unit map and Incident Action Plan map.

Two types of topographic maps include:

- Contour maps

Contour maps are the most common way to show the shape and elevation of the land (Figure 1-2). A contour is an imaginary line, where all points on the line are at the same elevation (above or below a specific reference elevation, usually sea level). Contour lines reveal the location of slopes, depressions, ridges, cliffs, and other topographical features.

Figure 1-2. Topographic map showing contours.

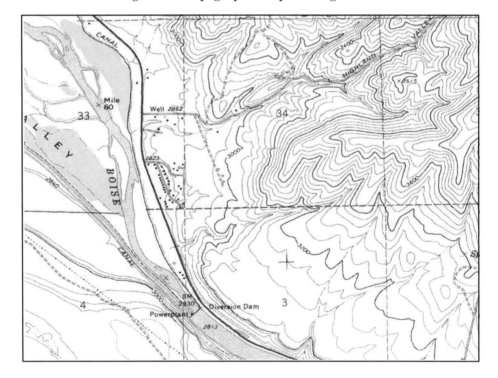

- Shaded-relief maps

Shaded-relief maps use a shadow effect color to simulate the terrain (Figure 1-3). Different color shades are used to accentuate the shape of the physical features. The darker the shading, the steeper the slope.

Figure 1-3. Shaded-relief map.

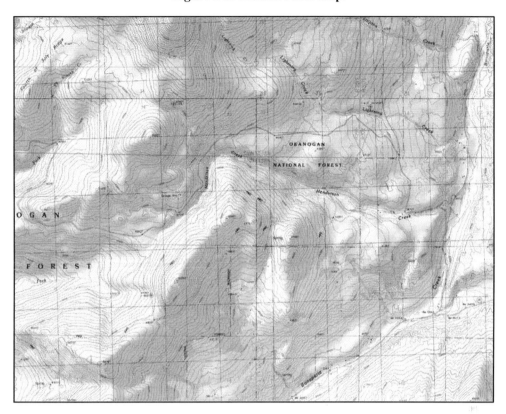

Orthophoto Maps

An orthophoto map is an aerial color-enhanced photograph of the land depicting terrain and other features (Figure 1-4).

Some orthophoto maps are overlain with contour lines and other features commonly associated with topographic maps. These maps are corrected for scale and are the same size as USGS topographic quadrangle maps.

Figure 1-4. Orthophoto map.

Incident Specific Maps

There are several different types of maps used on an incident and they each have their own specific purpose.

Situation Unit Map

The Situation Unit map is the most current map of the incident because it is continuously updated (Figure 1-5).

It is the master map and other incident maps are often derived from this map. The Situation Unit map is a large topographic map that is computer generated or hand drawn.

Figure 1-5. Situation Unit map.

Incident Action Plan (IAP) Map

The Incident Action Plan map is the primary map that operations personnel use to accomplish the incident mission. It represents a snapshot in time and is published daily in the IAP. It is a small, black and white topographic map (typically 8½" x 11" or 11" x 17") that is hand-drawn or computer generated (Figures 1-6 and 1-7). It contains the same information that is on the Situation Unit map.

Figure 1-6. Incident Action Plan map (hand-drawn).

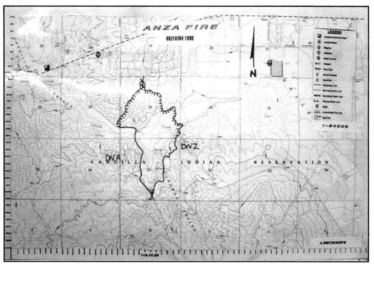

Figure 1-7. Incident Action Plan map (computer generated).

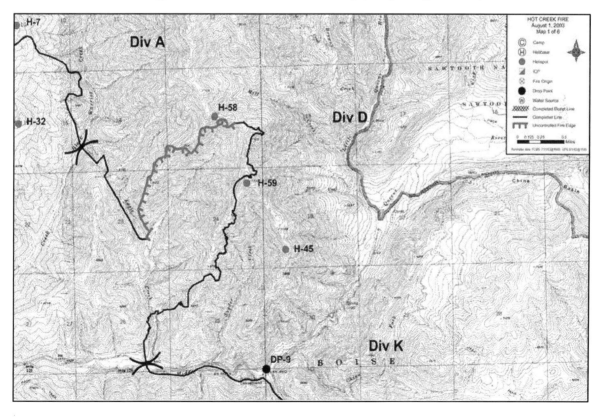

Operational Briefing Map

The Operational Briefing map is used during briefings to discuss work assignments and other details for the upcoming operational period (Figure 1-8).

Figure 1-8. Operational Briefing map.

Progression Map

The Progression map shows how the incident has grown over the landscape according to a time scale and is used to track the incident's progression (Figure 1-9). It is a topographic or shaded-relief map that illustrates the changing perimeter, which is distinguishable by color or text. The size of the Progression map varies.

Figure 1-9. Progression map.

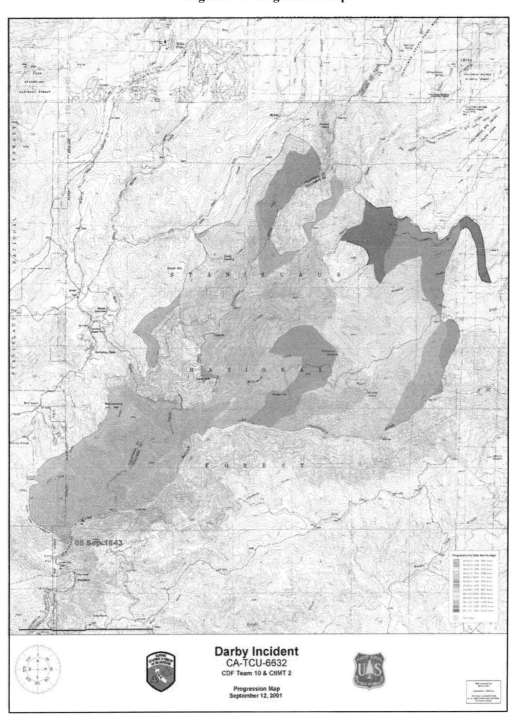

Facilities Map

The Facilities map is used to orient incident staff to the layout of the incident command post and camp (Figure 1-10). It is typically on one page, 8½" x 11", and included in the IAP.

Figure 1-10. Facilities map.

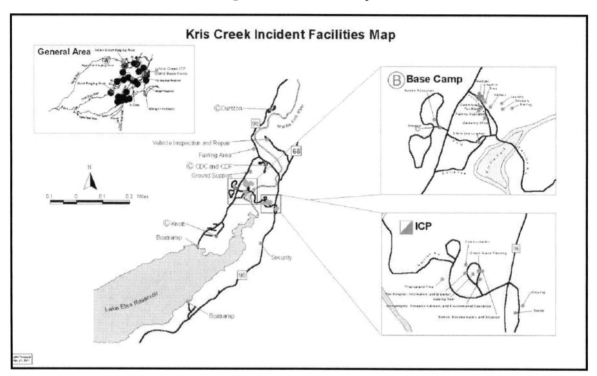

Transportation Map

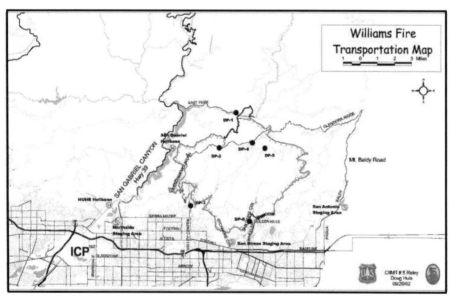

This map shows travel routes and overall access to the incident (Figure 1-11).

It is used to facilitate the safe delivery of equipment, supplies, and personnel to and from the incident location.

It is typically 8½" x 11" and included in the IAP.

Infrared Map

Infrared maps display heat sources and hot spots on a fire incident (Figure 1-12).

Infrared Interpreters (IRIN) translate information from infrared imagery to the topographic maps. Several shades of black and white are used to depict heat sources. Black represents the hottest spots while white shows the cooler areas.

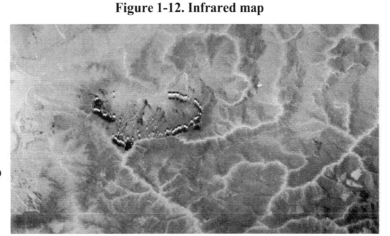

Figure 1-12. Infrared map

Structure Protection Map

This map displays locations of improvements (e.g., structures) in relationship to the incident.

Air Operations Map

This is a topographic or shaded-relief map with symbology that pertains to air operations. It may include temporary flight restrictions and flight hazards.

Public Information Map

This map is used to keep the public informed and does not show tactical details. It shows incident location in relationship to communities and other points of interest.

Fire History Map

The fire history map displays fire perimeter in relationship to previously burned areas.

Ownership Map

This map displays land ownership within and adjacent to the incident perimeter.

Rehabilitation Map

The rehabilitation map displays incident activities that may cause environmental impacts. This map also charts progress of rehabilitation activities.

Fuels/Vegetation Map

This map displays fuels and/or vegetation within and adjacent to the incident perimeter.

Map Legend and Symbols

Most maps have a legend that is used to interpret symbols on the map such as what color line delineates a road or land ownership boundary, or what symbol represents a building, stream, or heliport (Figure 1-13). The symbols used vary with every map, depending upon the purpose of the map. The legend may also include the map scale and other important information.

Figure 1-13. Example of a map legend.

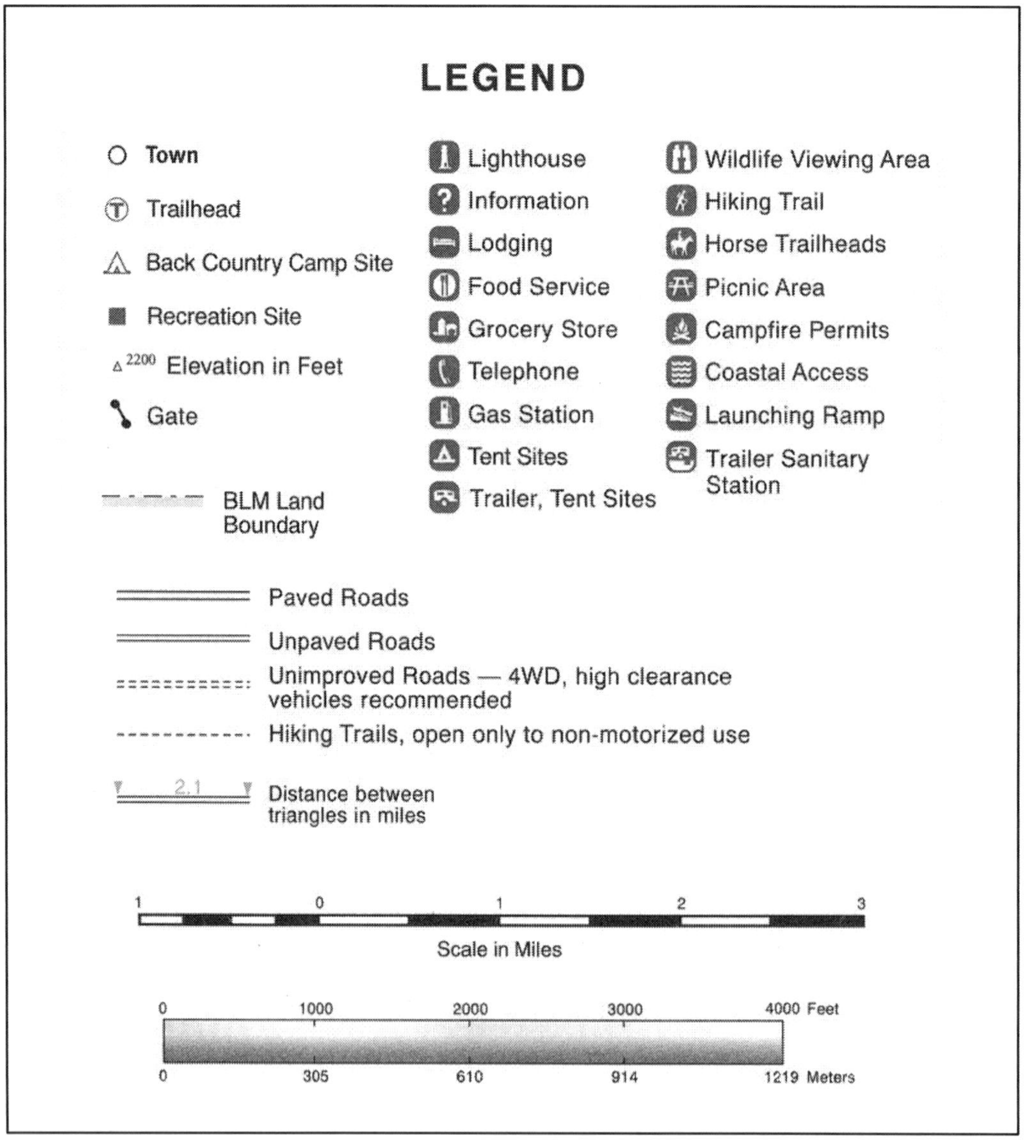

Symbol Colors

Map symbols are usually printed in colors with each color representing a class of features. The colors and features used on incident maps include:

- Blue – facilities, water

- Red – fire features, origin, roads

- Black – roads, control lines, drop points

- Orange – fire spread prediction

- Green – vegetation

- Brown – contours, cuts and fills, other relief features

- Purple – revised information

- Grey – developed areas

- Other colors may be used for special purposes.

Types of Symbols

Incident Command System (ICS) has a standardized, color-coded symbol set that was developed specifically for the ICS (Figure 1-14). Additional symbols can be created for incident maps, but they must be defined in the legend.

Figure 1-14. Incident Command System symbology.

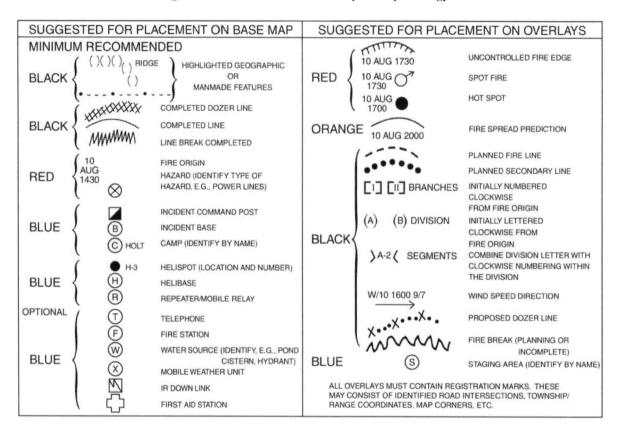

Map Sources

There are several different places to obtain maps.

Federal Agencies – Local, Regional, and National Offices

The local, regional, and national offices for federal agencies often have maps for their specific jurisdiction.

Local/State Agency Offices

Local and state agency offices (forestry, fire, police, emergency management) will have maps of the local area.

Local Business Offices

Local business offices (real estate, contractors, utility companies, Chamber of Commerce) may also have maps of the local area.

Internet

Several agencies have statewide data sets available online.

Mapping Software

Mapping software is now available that offers a variety of features, such as printing maps, plotting points, determining acreage, and downloading GPS information (tracks, waypoints, routes). Geographic Information System is the major software system that is used for mapping data; however, there are other software products available.

This page intentionally left blank.

Checking Your Understanding

Answers to "Checking Your Understanding" can be found in Appendix B.

1.	List three examples of how you may use a map on an incident.

2.	Describe two key points to remember when using a map with a compass or GPS receiver.

3.	Indicate the type of map that would be most appropriate for these activities:

Λ.	Locate hot spots on an incident – _____

B.	Determine slope of a specific area – _____

C.	Identify travel route – _____

D.	Determine current perimeter location – _____

E.	Identify perimeter location when the incident started – _____

4.	What publication can you use to learn the ICS symbols?

5.	List three sources of where you can obtain maps.

This page intentionally left blank

Chapter 2 – READING TOPOGRAPHIC MAPS AND MAKING CALCULATIONS

In this chapter you will learn about:

- ➢ Reading the margins
- ➢ Interpreting contour lines
- ➢ Estimating slope
- ➢ Estimating aspect
- ➢ Estimating acreage
- ➢ Estimating distances
- ➢ Estimating percent contained

A nice reference to have while reading this chapter is a USGS color topographic map.

A topographic map is printed on a flat piece of paper yet it provides a picture of the terrain and man-made features through the use of contour lines, colors and symbols. Contour lines represent the shape and elevation of the land, such as ridges, valleys, and hills. Colors and symbols are used to represent other features on the land, such as water, vegetation, roads, boundaries, urban areas and structures.

The USGS produces a series of topographic maps that are extremely accurate. The United States was systematically divided into precise quadrangles based on latitude and longitude lines and these maps are commonly referred to as "quads."

This chapter starts with tips on how to read the margins of a topographic map. Then it describes how to interpret contour lines. Finally, it covers how to estimate slope, aspect, acreage, distances, and percent contained using a topographic map.

Reading the Margins

This section addresses how to read the information that is in the margins of a USGS topographic map. It starts with the upper left corner of the map and moves clockwise around the map.

Agency or Author Who Created Map (upper left corner of map)

In Figure 2-1, the United States Department of the Interior Geological Survey is the agency that created the map. This same information can also be found in the bottom left corner.

Figure 2-1. Agency or author who created map.

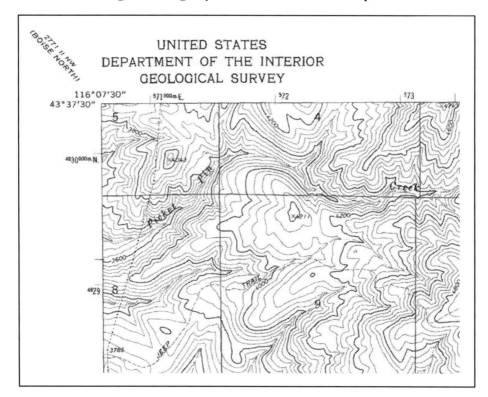

Map Title (upper right corner of map)

This corner section provides the name of quadrangle, state (and sometimes the county) where the quadrangle is located, and map series. Quadrangles are often named after a prominent town or feature that is in the quadrangle. In Figure 2-2, the name of the quadrangle is "Lucky Peak" which is located in Idaho. The map series indicates how much land area is on the map; for example, in Figure 2-2 the Lucky Peak quadrangle is a 7.5 minute series which indicates it covers a four sided area of 7.5 minutes of latitude and 7.5 minutes of longitude.

Figure 2-2. Map title.

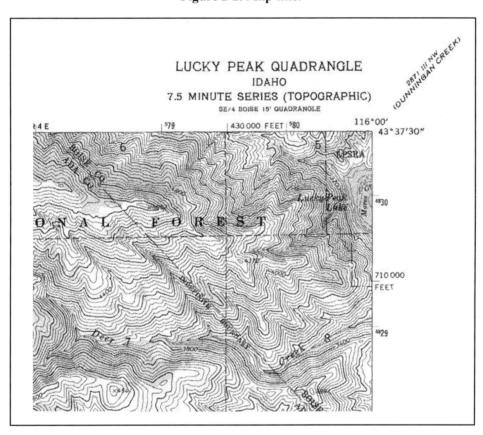

Road Classification (bottom right corner of map)

Road and trail symbols may be found in this legend (Figure 2-3).

Revision Date (bottom right corner of map)

Some maps have a revision date, which is when the map was last updated. If the map is old, it may not be accurate. In Figure 2-3 the revision date is 1972. Refer to the "Map Production Information" block in the bottom left corner for additional information on map dates.

Quadrangle Location (bottom right corner of map)

The location of the quadrangle is pinpointed on a map of the state (Figure 2-3).

Adjoining Quadrangle Legend (corners of map)

Names of adjoining quadrangles are frequently indicated in the corner margins of USGS topographical maps; *Mayfield* is the joining quadrangle in Figure 2-3.

Figure 2-3. Road classification, revision date, quadrangle location and adjoining maps.

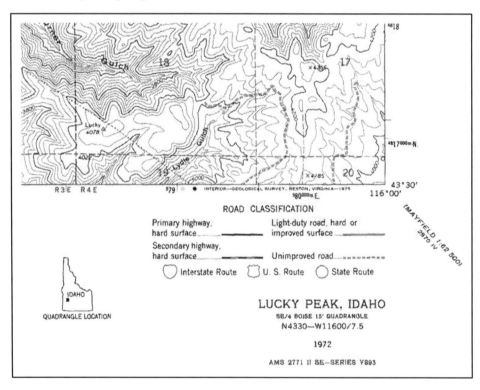

Some topographic maps will have an adjoining quadrangle legend (Figure 2-4).

Figure 2-4. Example of an adjoining quadrangle legend.

1	2	3	1. NORTHEAST EMMETT 2. MONTOUR 3. HORSESHOE BEND
4	PEARL	5	4. SOUTHEAST EMMETT 5. CARTWRIGHT CANYON
6	7	8	6. STAR 7. EAGLE 8. BOISE NORTH

Map Scale (bottom center of map)

The map scale indicates the ratio or proportion of the horizontal distance on the map to the corresponding horizontal distance on the ground (Figure 2-5).

Figure 2-5. Map scale (fractional scale and bar scale) and contour interval.

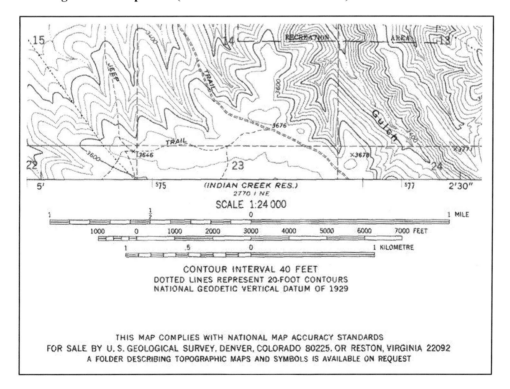

There are two types of scales on the topographic map:

- Fractional Scale

  The fractional scale expresses the ratio of the map distance to the ground distance in **like** units of measurements. It is usually written as a fraction or ratio. For example, the map in Figure 2-5 has a map scale of 1:24,000 which means one inch on the map is 24,000 inches on the ground.

  Typically, USGS produces maps using the 1:24,000 scale, but will also produce maps using 1:62,500 and 1:250,000 scale. The 1:24,000 scale provides larger and clearer details than the 1:250,000, but it does not cover as large an area.

  The maps produced at a 1:24,000 scale (1 inch represents 24,000 inches or 2000 feet) are commonly known as 7.5-minute quadrangle maps; each map covers 7.5 minutes of latitude and 7.5 minutes of longitude, which is approximately 8 miles (north/south) and 6 miles (east/west). The primary scale used in Alaska topographic maps is 1:63,360 (1 inch represents 1 mile) due to the size of the state. The Alaska quadrangle map covers 15 minutes of latitude and varies from 20 – 36 minutes of longitude.

- Bar or Graphic Scale

  A graphic scale or comparison scale is entirely different from the representative fraction scale. It usually compares map distances to the ground distance in **different** units of measurements.

  Usually a graphic scale is a line marked off on a map indicating so many inches or millimeters equal to so many feet, kilometers, chains, or miles on the ground. A comparison scale of 1 inch to 2000 feet means that 1 inch on the map is proportioned to 2000 feet on the ground. We are comparing inches and feet which are **different units** of measurement.

Contour Interval (bottom center of the map)

Contour interval is the difference in elevation between two adjacent contour lines. In Figure 2-5, the contour interval is 40 feet. On USGS maps, contour intervals are usually 1, 5, 10, 20, 40, and 80 feet. If the contour interval is not printed on the map it can be calculated (which is discussed later in this chapter).

North Arrow, Declination, and Map Production Information (bottom left corner of map)

It is common practice for maps to be oriented with true north at the top. Most USGS maps have a symbol of arrows pointing to the geographic North Pole (shown by a star), magnetic north (MN) and grid north (GN). Grid north shows the difference between geographic north (latitude/longitude) and the UTM grid.

In Figure 2-6, the magnetic north is 18.5 degrees east. The difference between the geographic North Pole and magnetic north is the magnetic declination for that map.

Figure 2-6. North arrow and magnetic declination.

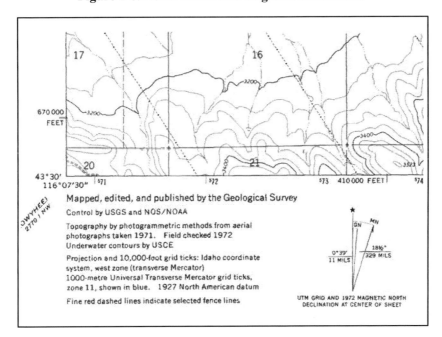

If the declination is not indicated on the arrow diagram, it can be found in the "Map Production Information" which is in the lower left corner of the map (Figure 2-7). The map production information section provides additional information on how and when the map was created. Sometimes the magnetic declination is printed here.

Figure 2-7. Map production information block often includes revision dates, datum, and UTM zone.

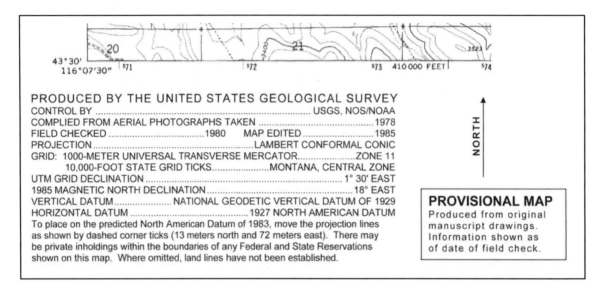

Datum and UTM Zone

The datum and UTM zone, which are extremely important when using a GPS receiver, can also be found in this block (Figure 2-7). Vertical and horizontal datums may be listed on the map; however, if the map lists only one datum then the vertical and the horizontal datum are the same.

Latitude and Longitude (edges of map)

Latitude and longitude lines are indicated with fine black tick marks along the edges of the map (Figure 2-8). Topographic maps do not show the latitude/longitude lines – just the tick marks. The numbers next to the tick marks indicate degrees (°), minutes (') and seconds ("). On 1:24,000 scale maps, latitude and longitude tick marks are indicated every 2.5 minutes.

- Longitude tick marks are on the top and bottom edges of the map and latitude tick marks are on the right and left edges. Note that the degrees may be left off (as an abbreviation) and you may only see the minute and/or second designations.

- Reference coordinates for latitude and longitude (degrees, minutes, and seconds) are black and located on the four corners of the map.

- The intersection of latitude and longitude lines are noted by cross-marks (+).

When reading latitude/longitude, pay close attention to the units (degrees, minutes, seconds) because it is easy to misread them. Refer to Chapters 3 and 6 for additional information on latitude and longitude.

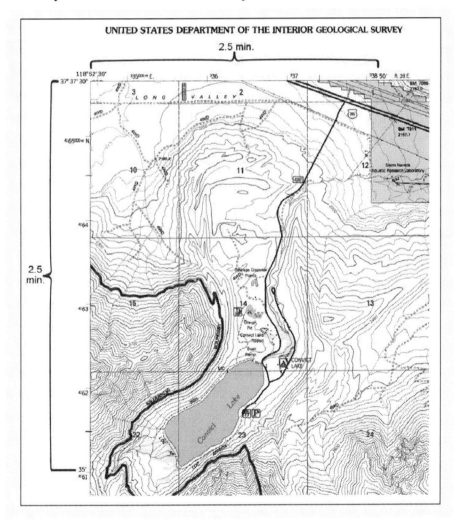

Figure 2-8.
Longitude tick marks (50'),
latitude tick marks (35'),
reference coordinates
(118° 52' 30" and 37° 37' 30"),
and cross-mark (+) in bottom
right corner.

Universal Transverse Mercator (UTM) (edges of map)

Prior to 1978, USGS topographic maps used blue tick marks along the edge of the map to illustrate where the UTM grid lines were located. Since 1978, USGS topographic maps actually show UTM grid lines (black) on the map and the coordinate values are in the margin. On USGS topographic maps, 7.5 quadrangle, the UTM grid lines are marked at 1,000 meter increments (Figure 2-9).

- Abbreviated easting values, for example ^{3}**36**, are located on the top and bottom edges of the map.

- Abbreviated northing values, for example ^{41}**64**, are located on the right and left edges of the map.

- Reference coordinates for UTM are located near the southeast and northwest corners of the map. Notice that the large bold numbers increase as you go north and east.

Refer to Chapters 3 and 6 for additional information on UTM.

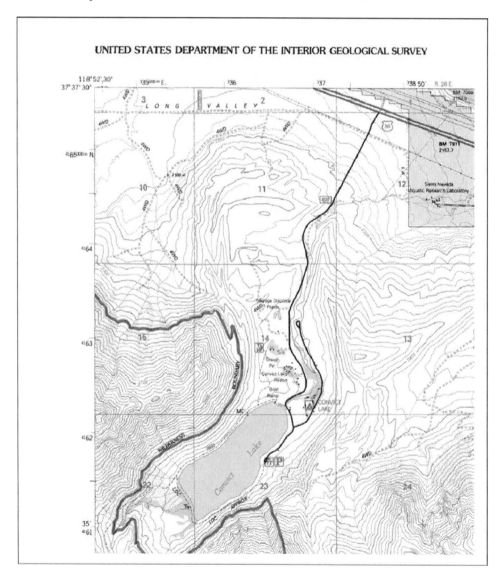

Figure 2-9. Easting (^{3}36, ^{3}37, ^{3}38) and northing (^{41}64, ^{41}63, ^{41}62, ^{41}61) value tick marks and reference coordinates (^{3}35^{000m}E. and ^{41}65^{000m}N.).

Section, Township, and Range (edges of map)

Section, township, and range numbers are red.

- Section numbers may be printed along the edge, but they are typically printed in the center of the section. In Figure 2-10, some of the section numbers include 15, 16, 17, 18, 19.

- Township numbers are printed along the right and left edge of the map. In Figure 2-10, the township numbers are T.2S and T.3S.

- Range numbers are printed on the top and bottom edge of the map. In Figure 2-10, the range numbers are R.1E and R.2E.

Refer to Chapter 3 for additional information on section, township, and range.

Figure 2-10. Sections, townships, and range.

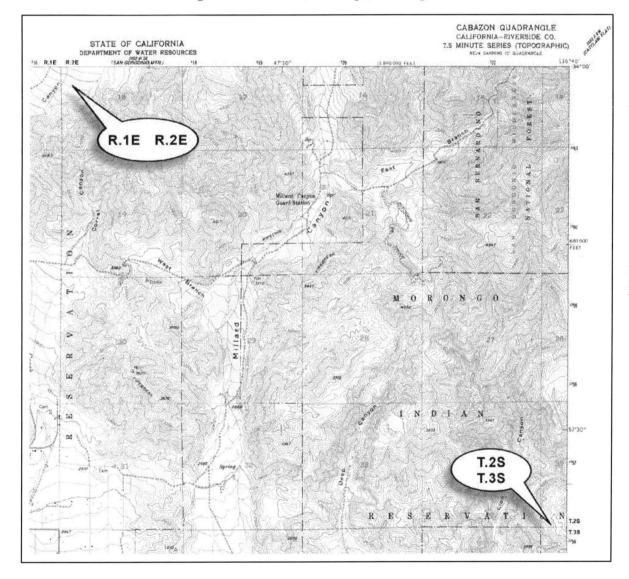

Interpreting Contour Lines

Contour lines on a map show topography or changes in elevation. They reveal the location of slopes, depressions, ridges, cliffs, height of mountains and hills, and other topographical features. A contour line is a brown line on a map that connects all points of the same elevation. They tend to parallel each other, each approximately the shape of the one above it and the one below it. In Figure 2-11, compare the topographic map with the landscape perspective.

Figure 2-11. A contour map and what it looks like from a landscape perspective. Note that contour lines are far apart for level land and almost touch for cliffs.

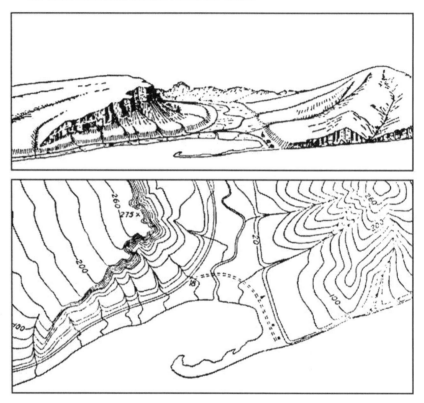

Contour Characteristics

Contours have general characteristics; some of which are illustrated in Figures 2-12 and 2-13.

- Concentric circles of contour lines indicate a hill.

- Evenly spaced contours indicate uniform slope.

- Widely spaced contours indicate a gentle slope.

- Widely spaced contours at the top of a hill indicate flat hilltop.

- Close together contours indicate steep slope, wall, or cliff.

- Close together contours at the top of a hill indicate a pointed hilltop.

- Crossing or touching contours indicate overhanging cliff.

**Figure 2-12. Evenly and widely spaced contours
indicate type of slope and shape of hilltop.**

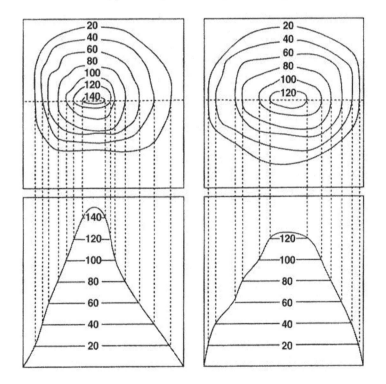

- Jagged, rough contours indicate large outcrops of rocks, cliffs, and fractured areas.

- "V" shape contours indicate stream beds and narrow valleys with the point of the "V" pointing uphill or upstream.

- "U" shape contours indicate ridges with the bottom of the "U" pointing down the ridge. A saddle is a ridge between two hills or summits.

- "M" or "W" shape contours indicate upstream from stream junctions.

- Circles with hachures or hatch lines (short lines extending from the contour line at right angles) indicate a depression, pit, or sinkhole.

- Spot elevations (height of identifiable features) such as mountain summits, road intersections, and surfaces of lakes may also be shown on the map.

Figure 2-13. Contour lines and topographic features.

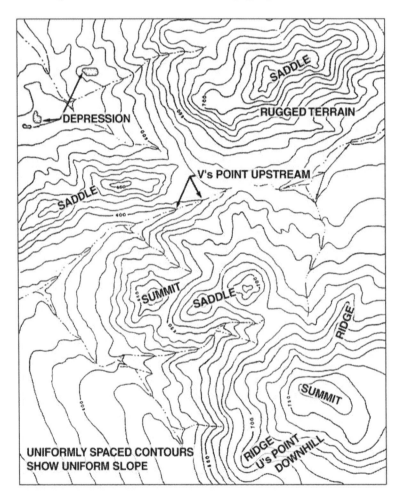

Chapter 2 – Basic Land Navigation

Contour Interval

Contour interval is the difference in elevation between two adjacent contour lines. On USGS maps, contour intervals are usually 1, 5, 10, 20, 40, and 80 feet. Occasionally you will find a map with a 25 foot contour interval or metric units, but not often. To make the contours easier to read, every fifth one is the **index contour** which is printed darker and has the elevation in feet from mean sea level marked on the line (Figure 2-14). The thinner or lighter colored contour lines are called **intermediate contours**.

Figure 2-14. Topographic map showing elevation of two index contours (700 and 800).

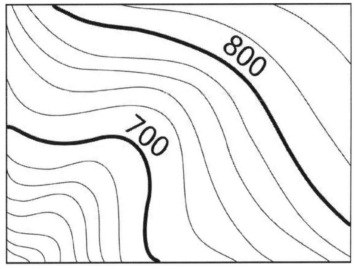

The contour interval is typically printed at the bottom of the map; however, if the contour interval is unknown, there is a way it can be calculated. Follow the steps in Table 2-1 to calculate the contour interval of the topographic map below.

Table 2-1. Calculating the contour interval

Steps	Directions
1	Find two index contours near each other: The index contours marked **4400** and **4600.**
2	Determine the **difference** in elevation between the two index contours: 4600 ft. – 4400 ft. = **200 ft.**
3	Count the number of contour lines between the two index contours: There are **5** lines. **Note:** There are actually 4 contour lines between the two index contours, but you always count one of the index contours as well as all of the contours in between.
4	Divide the difference (step 2) by the number of lines (step 3): 200 ft. ÷ 5 = **40 ft.** This is the contour interval.

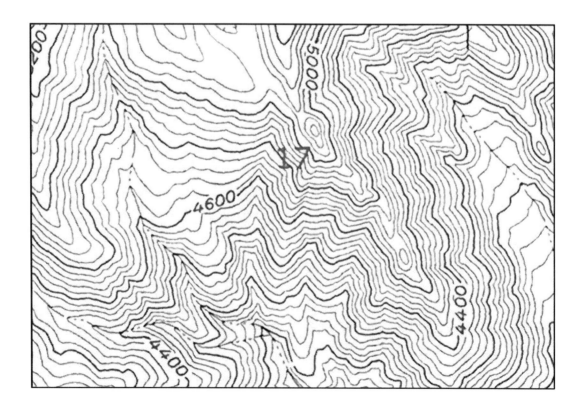

Estimating Slope

Slope is used by the operations section in several different ways: to estimate the amount of time it takes to construct a fireline; to determine whether or not a dozer, engine, or hand crew can work in a specific area; to calculate pump pressure needed to reach a location; and to calculate fire behavior characteristics, such as rate of spread.

On incidents, slope is the degree of inclination or steepness and it is usually expressed in percent. A one percent slope indicates a rise or drop of one unit over a distance of 100 horizontal units.

For example, a one percent slope rise would indicate a one foot rise over a 100 foot horizontal distance. Slope can be calculated using a topographic map or it can be determined in the field with a clinometer (see Chapter 4, Using a Compass and Clinometer).

To calculate slope using a topographic map, you will need to determine the following:

- Vertical Distance (also referred to as Rise) – This is the difference in elevation between two points; it is calculated by subtracting the elevation of one point from the elevation of the other point.

- Horizontal Distance (also referred to as Run) – This is the distance from one point to the other and is calculated by measuring distance with a ruler and applying the map scale. For example, if the map scale is 1:24,000 and the distance between the two points when measured with a ruler is ½ inch, the horizontal distance would be 12,000 inches or 1,000 feet.

Slope can then be calculated using the slope formula:

$$\frac{\text{Vertical Distance}}{\text{Horizontal Distance}} \times 100 = \% \text{ Slope}$$

Another way to write the slope formula is:

$$\frac{\text{Rise}}{\text{Run}} \times 100 = \% \text{ Slope}$$

There are a number of slope calculation aids in the form of tables that show the relationship between map scale and contour interval. Be careful when using slope calculation aids because they are tailored to specific map scales and contour intervals.

Follow the steps in Table 2-2 to estimate the percent of slope between the two points on the topographic map below.

Table 2-2. Steps to estimate slope between two points.

Steps	Directions
1	The contour interval is 20ft.
2	The elevation of point A is 9440 ft. and point B is 9640 ft.
3	Determine the vertical distance (or rise) between the two points by subtracting the elevation of point A from the elevation of point B (200 ft.).
4	Use a ruler to measure the horizontal distance (or run) between the two points (½ inch). Use the map scale (1:24,000) to convert the ½ inch into feet (1000 ft.).
5	Compute the percentage of the slope using the slope formula: 200 ft. ÷ 1000 ft. = .20 Slope is 20%

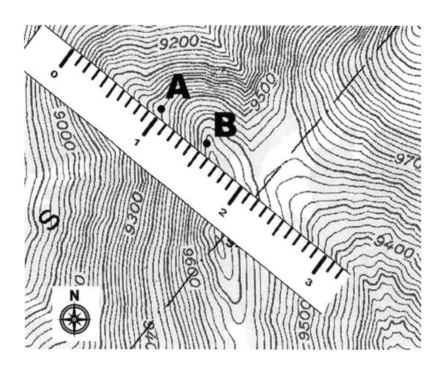

Estimating Aspect

Aspect is the compass direction that the slope is facing. On a topographic map, use index contour lines (they will tell you the difference in elevation) and the north arrow to determine which direction the slope is facing. Follow the steps in Table 2-3 to estimate aspect of the slope between the two points on the topographic map below.

Table 2-3. Steps to estimate aspect.

Steps	Directions
1	Determine the elevation of point A (9480 ft.) and point B (9680 ft.).
2	Since point B is a higher elevation than point A, the terrain is sloping from point B down to point A.
3	Use the north arrow on the map to determine which direction the slope is facing, which is northwest. The aspect is northwest.

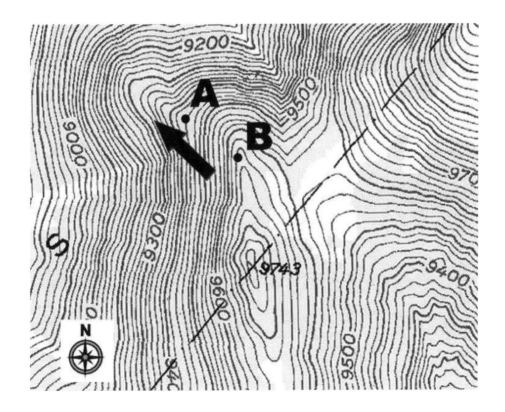

Estimating Acreage

Area can be expressed in square miles, acres, blocks, square feet, or any other square unit of linear measurement. This section discusses different methods for estimating acreage (area formula, dot grid, planimeter, comparison, and GPS receiver). Refer to the Wildland Fire Incident Management Field Guide (PMS 210), for additional information on estimating acreage.

Area Formula

The most common method for calculating area is using the formula: length x width = area.

Area is always calculated in square measure, and the answer will be in square units (square feet, square yards, square chains). When calculating area, typical units of measurements include:

- Linear units of measurement

12 inches	=	1 foot
3 feet	=	1 yard
5280 feet	=	1 mile
66 feet	=	1 chain
80 chains	=	1 mile
3.2808 feet =		1 meter

- Area units of measurement

1 acre	=	208 feet x 208 feet
1 acre	=	43,560 square feet
1 acre	=	10 square chains
640 acres	=	1 square mile
1 section	=	1 square mile*
1/2 section	=	320 acres*
1/4 section	=	160 acres*
1 hectare	=	2.4 acres

*Generally the size, but may vary due to surveying deviations.

Following are three examples of how to estimate acreage using the area formula:

1. What is the acreage if the length is 2,640 feet and width is 1,320 feet? Remember that 43,560 square feet equals one acre.

Table 2-4. Estimate acreage using feet.

Steps	Directions
1	Multiply the length by the width to get the area: 2640 ft. x 1320 ft. = 3,484,800 sq. ft.
2	Convert the 3,484,800 sq. ft. to acres: 3,484,800 sq. ft. x $\dfrac{1 \text{ acre}}{43,560 \text{ sq. ft.}}$ = 80 acres

2. What is the acreage if the length is 5 chains and width is 10 chains? Remember that 10 square chains equals one acre.

Table 2-5. Estimate acreage using chains.

Steps	Directions
1	Multiply the length by the width to get the area: 5 chains x 10 chains = 50 square chains
2	Convert the 50 square chains to acres: 50 square chains x $\dfrac{1 \text{ acre}}{10 \text{ chains}}$ = 5 acres

3. What is the acreage for an odd shaped area that is 32 chains wide at one end, 16 chains wide at the other end, and 48 chains in length?

Table 2-6. Estimate acreage for an odd shaped area.

Steps	Directions
1	Multiply the length by the width to get the area: 48 chains x $\dfrac{16 + 32}{2}$ chains = 1152 square chains Note: To estimate the acreage for an odd shaped area, it is often necessary to take two or more measurements across the area and obtain an <u>average</u> length and width. The <u>average</u> width is obtained by adding the two different widths (16 + 32) and dividing by 2.
2	Convert the 1152 square chains to acres: 1152 square chains x $\dfrac{1\ acre}{10\ chains}$ = 115.2 acres

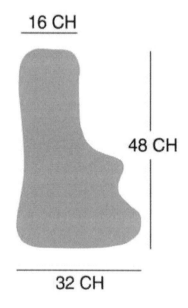

16 CH

48 CH

32 CH

Dot Grid

A dot grid is an inexpensive and readily available tool that is used to estimate acreage (Figure 2-15). There are many different types of dot grids. Each dot represents a specific number of acres depending upon the map scale. For example, if you are using the dot grid in Figure 2-16 on a 7.5 minute quad map, each dot represents 1.434 acres, while on a 15 minute quad map, each dot represents 9.73 acres.

Figure 2-15. A dot grid is used to estimate acreage.

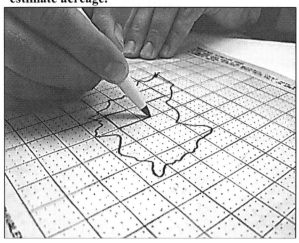

Figure 2-16. This is one example of a dot grid (not to scale).

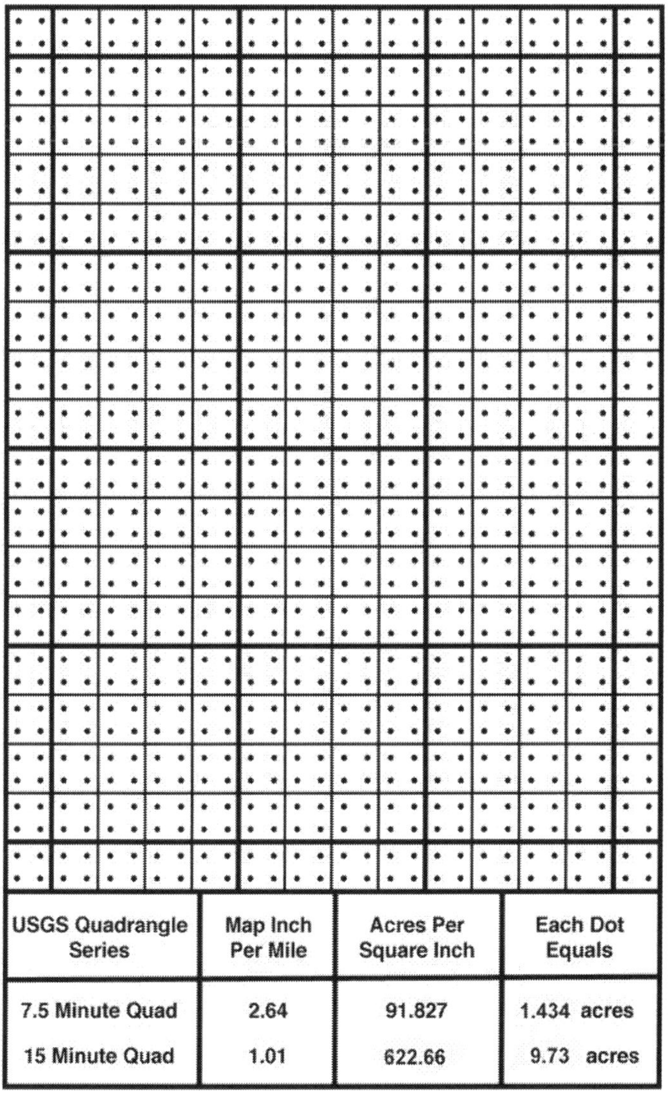

USGS Quadrangle Series	Map Inch Per Mile	Acres Per Square Inch	Each Dot Equals
7.5 Minute Quad	2.64	91.827	1.434 acres
15 Minute Quad	1.01	622.66	9.73 acres

If a dot grid has no scale or you are working with a map where the scale is questionable, it will be necessary to calibrate the dot grid – which means you need to determine how many acres each dot represents. Table 2-7 describes how to calibrate a dot grid.

Table 2-7. Steps for calibrating a dot grid

Steps	Directions
1	Determine **map scale.** For this example, we will use a map scale of 1:24000 (1 inch = 2,000 feet).
2	Calculate **acres per square inch.** This will often involve using the conversion: 1 acre = 43,560 square feet. Example: 1 inch = 2,000 feet 2,000 ft. x 2,000 ft. = 4,000,000 sq. ft. $4,000,000 \text{ sq. ft.} \times \dfrac{1 \text{ acre}}{43,560 \text{ sq. ft.}} = 91.8 \text{ acres per sq. inch}$
3	Determine **acres per dot.** First determine the number of dots per square inch that are on the dot grid. For this example, there are 64 dots per square inch. $\dfrac{91.8 \text{ acres}}{\text{sq. in.}} \times \dfrac{\text{sq. in.}}{64 \text{ (dots)}} = 1.434 \text{ acres per dot}$

Table 2-8 describes how to use a dot grid to estimate the acreage of the fire illustrated below.

Table 2-8. Steps for estimating acreage using a dot grid.

Steps	Directions
1	Place the dot grid over the incident perimeter; the position of the dot grid isn't important.
2	Count all the dots that fall completely within the incident perimeter. Record the number.
3	Count every other dot that falls on the boundary of the incident perimeter. Record the number.
4	Add dot counts from steps 2 and 3. This cumulative number of dots represents the total area being measured. Multiply the total count by the area represented by one dot to arrive at the area measurement. In the example below, each dot equals 1.434 acres. 63 (approximate dot count) x 1.434 acres (area represented by one dot) = 90.3 acres

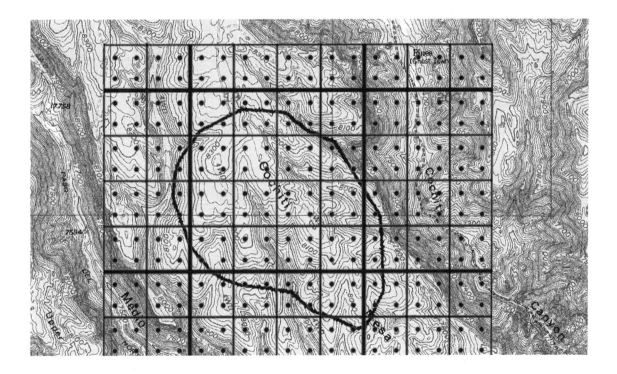

Planimeter

A planimeter is a tool that can be used to measure acreage on a map (Figure 2-17). Use the planimeter to trace around the perimeter a number of times to obtain an average acreage.

Figure 2-17. Planimeter

Comparison

Another way to estimate the size of an area is by comparing it to areas of a known size. For example, if the area is entirely within a single section then it can be safe to assume it isn't more than 640 acres; if it is the size of a football field the estimate would be one acre.

Global Positioning System (GPS) Receiver

Several models of GPS receivers have the ability to calculate area (acreage).

Estimating Distances

Refer to the map scale for measuring distances on the map. On 7.5 minute quad topographic maps the engineer's 20 scale ruler is a nice tool because 20 graduations on the ruler equals 1 inch which equals 2,000 feet.

To calculate distances you will need a map wheel (Figure 2-18), string, paper with tick marks, or other measuring tool. A map wheel has a toothed wheel and as it moves it measures distances on maps. Set the map wheel's scale to match the map's scale and then roll the wheel along the route to be measured. Table 2-9 describes the steps to estimate distances using a map wheel.

Figure 2-18. There are different types of map wheels.

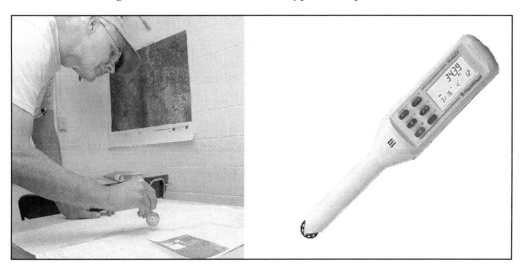

Table 2-9. Steps for estimating distances using a map wheel.

Steps	Directions
1	Set map wheel to zero and calibrate using scale on the map.
2	Roll the map wheel along the distance to be estimated. Do this twice or more to get an average.

Estimating Percent Contained

To estimate percent contained, use this formula:

$$\frac{\text{Completed line distance}}{\text{Perimeter distance}} \times 100 = \text{Percent contained}$$

This page intentionally left blank.

Chapter 2 – Basic Land Navigation

Checking Your Understanding

Answers to "Checking Your Understanding" can be found in Appendix B.

1. What is the fractional scale and declination of this map? If you are using a GPS receiver, what datum would you use?

    Fractional scale:_____

    Declination:_____

    Datum:_____

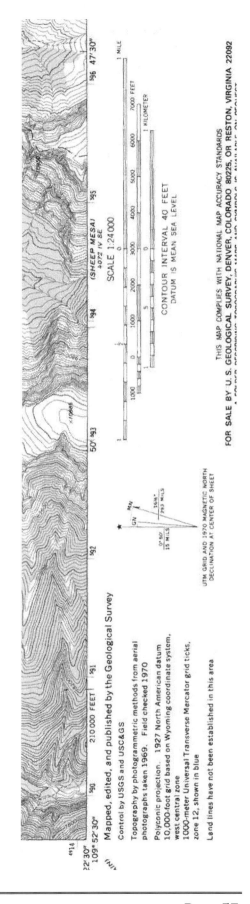

2. List the reference coordinates for latitude/longitude and UTM.

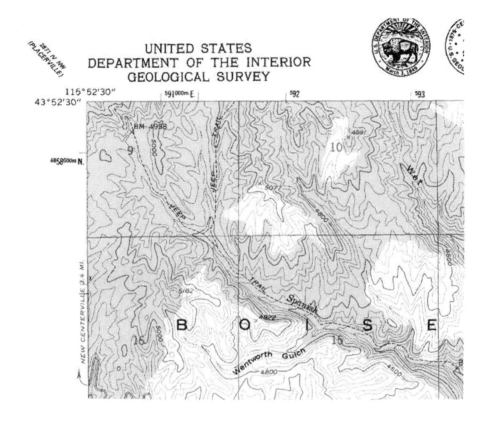

Reference coordinates latitude:_____

Reference coordinates longitude:_____

Reference coordinates UTM:_____

3. Calculate the contour interval for this map.

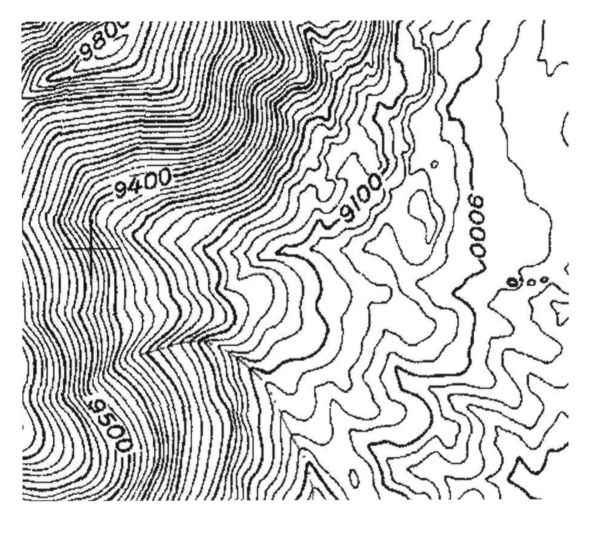

Contour interval: _____

4. Draw a profile (similar to a line graph) of the land from point "a" to point "b." Elevation lines are marked in 100-foot increments. Hint: The elevation rises from the 100-foot contour line.

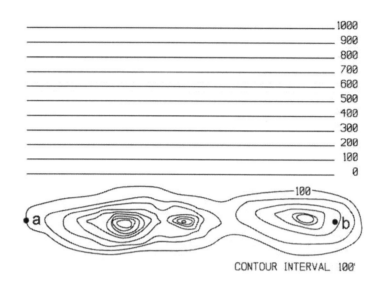

CONTOUR INTERVAL 100'

5. Use the map on the next page to identify the topographic feature inside the rectangles lettered A - F with one of these characteristics: stream, hilltop, steep terrain, ridge, depression, and flat terrain.

A. _____

B. _____

C. _____

D. _____

E. _____

F. _____

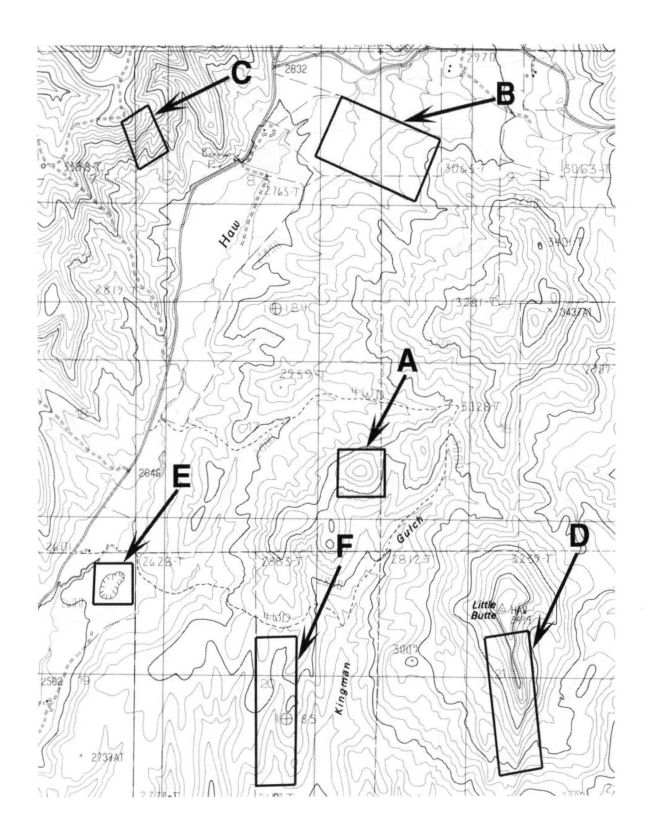

6. Estimate the percent slope between A and B. What is the aspect of the slope between A and B?
    The scale is 1:24,000 (1 inch = 2000 feet).

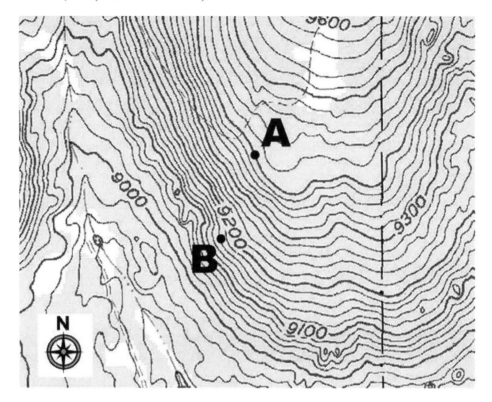

    Slope:_____   Aspect:_____

7. Determine the equivalent unit of measurement for the following:

    A.   2.5 miles   =_____chains

    B.   1.5 chains   =_____yards

    C.   29,040 feet   =_____miles

    D.   3 chains x 20 chains   =_____acres

    E.   1/8 of a section   =_____acres

8. Use the map on the next page to estimate the acreage (in acres) within 10% accuracy (+ or -) of
    fires A - D.

    A. _____

    B. _____

    C. _____

    D. _____

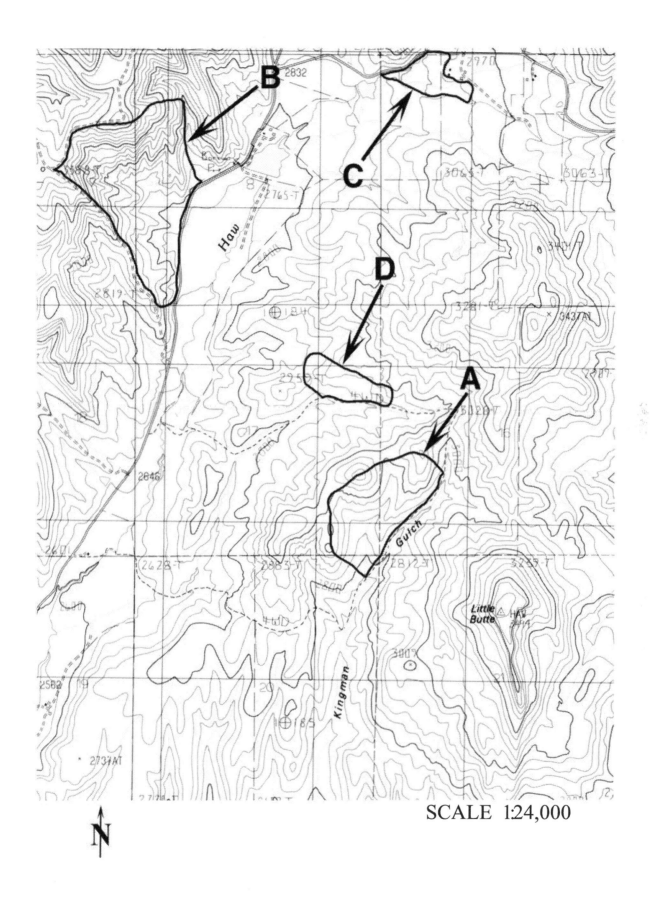

SCALE 1:24,000

This page intentionally left blank.

Chapter 2 – Basic Land Navigation

Chapter 3 – GEOGRAPHIC LOCATION SYSTEMS

In this chapter you will learn about:

➢ Latitude and longitude
➢ Universal Transverse Mercator (UTM)
➢ U.S. Public Land Survey
➢ Other geographic location systems

Geographic location systems or coordinate systems were developed as a tool to describe specific geographic locations and are used for navigation and mapping. Generally, they consist of a grid of imaginary intersecting lines which are used to describe a position on a map. Most of these systems use coordinate values, which are expressed as numeric or alphanumeric characters, to define geographic locations. Coordinate systems are based on reference points from which position measurements are made. For example, the reference points for latitude and longitude are the prime meridian and equator.

This chapter discusses two types of global geographic location systems commonly used in the United States – latitude/longitude and UTM. Then, it describes the U.S. Public Land Survey (section, township, and range) and other types of geographic location systems.

Refer to Chapter 6, Navigation and Field Mapping, for information on how to plot and map points using geographic location systems.

Latitude/Longitude

Latitude/longitude is a global system which precisely identifies locations using the equator as a reference point for latitude and the prime meridian as a reference point for longitude (Figure 3-1).

Figure 3-1. Latitude and longitude lines.

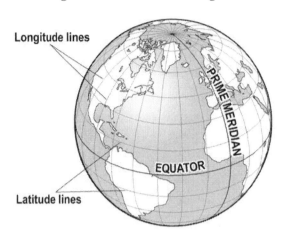

Latitude

Latitude lines circle the world parallel with the equator, running in an easterly and westerly direction. These lines are identified by their position either north or south of the equator. The equator is 0° latitude and the North Pole (90° N) and South Pole (90° S) are both 90° latitude. All other points on earth have latitudes ranging between 0° to 90° north or 0° to 90° south. When stating the position coordinates, latitude is always said first (Figure 3-2).

Longitude

Longitude lines run true north to true south – North Pole to South Pole. Longitude is the distance east or west of the prime meridian (Greenwich, England). The prime meridian is 0° longitude.

Figure 3-2. The coordinates for the point where latitude and longitude meet are described as 30°N, 50°W.

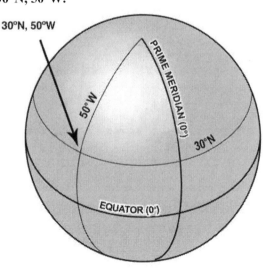

All other points on earth have longitudes ranging between 0° to 180° east and 0° to 180° west. Lines of longitude are not parallel; the closer they are to the poles, the shorter the distance between them. Principal meridian lines run in the same direction as the lines of longitude.

Latitude and Longitude Coordinates

There are three primary ways of describing locations using latitude and longitude coordinates:

1. Degrees Minutes Seconds (ddd° mm' ss.s")

    This is the most common format that is used on maps:

43° 23' 45"	71° 8' 36"
(Latitude)	(Longitude)

2. Degrees Decimal Minutes (ddd° mm.mmm')

    This format is used by aircraft guidance systems:

43° 23.75' Latitude	71° 8.6' Longitude

    On incidents, this system should be used by personnel to establish common terminology between incident personnel and air operations.

3. Decimal Degrees (ddd.dddd°)

    This is used by National Weather Service and other agencies, as well as some computer based mapping systems:

43.395833° Latitude	71.143333° Longitude

Counting and Converting Minutes and Seconds

When working with latitude and longitude, it is essential to know how to count minutes and seconds and be familiar with conversions. Counting minutes and seconds for latitude/longitude is the same as counting time on a clock. When the seconds count reaches 60, carry over and add 1 minute to the minute number in the coordinate, and start counting seconds again from 0. When the minute count reaches 60, carry 1 degree over and add it to the degrees number and start counting minutes again from 0.

If the point lies in the western hemisphere, count degrees, minutes and seconds from right to left (east to west).

Common conversions include:

> 60 seconds (60") = one minute (1')
> 60 minutes (60') = one degree (1°)
> 7.5 minutes = 1/8 of 60 minutes = 1/8 of a degree
> 15 minutes = ¼ of 60 minutes = ¼ of a degree
> 15 seconds = 0.25 minutes
> 30 seconds = 0.5 minutes
> 45 seconds = .75 minutes

To convert from **degrees minutes seconds to degrees decimal minutes** divide the seconds by 60 to get the decimal minutes, for example:

> 48° 20' 30" → 30" → 60 = .5 → 48° 20.5'

To convert **degrees decimal minutes to degrees minutes seconds** multiply the decimal (e.g., .5) by 60, for example:

> 48° 20.5' → .5 x 60 = 30" → 48° 20' 30"

Universal Transverse Mercator (UTM)

Universal Transverse Mercator is a global coordinate system that is defined in meters rather than degrees-minutes-seconds. UTM is a very precise method of defining geographic locations; therefore, it is commonly used in GPS and GIS mapping. When using the UTM coordinate system, a location can be identified within a meter.

UTM Grid Zones

The UTM grid divides the world into 60 north-south zones; the zones are numbered 1-60 (Figure 3-3). Each zone is 6 degrees wide in longitude. The contiguous 48 states has 10 zones. Within each zone is superimposed a square grid, and although the zone lines converge toward the poles, the grid lines do not. Therefore, as one travels north from the equator, the grid becomes smaller, although the grid squares remain the same.

Figure 3-3. Universal Transverse Mercator zones.

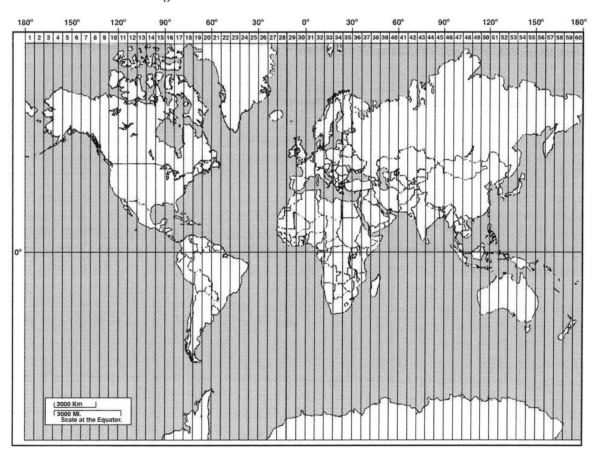

UTM Coordinates

UTM uses two coordinates – easting and northing – to determine a location. Locations within a zone are measured in meters east and west from the central meridian, and north and south from the equator (Figure 3-4).

Figure 3-4. Numbering system for UTM coordinates within a zone.

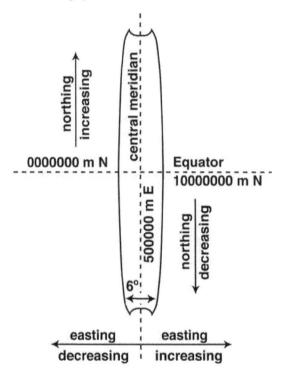

- Easting coordinate

The central meridian is an arbitrary line drawn down the center of each zone, and given a false easting value of 500,000 meters so that only positive eastings are measured anywhere in the zone. Eastings increase eastward and decrease westward from the central meridian. Each zone at its widest point cannot exceed 999,999 meters. As you move north and south from the equator, the zones become narrower, just like meridians of longitude, so, depending on where you are in relation to the equator, the east edge of each zone will end at different distances from the central meridian.

- Northing coordinate

Northing is the distance in meters north and south of the equator (measured along a zone line).

If the point lies north of the equator, coordinates always increase from south to north (bottom of map to the top) of the equator, with the equator given a value of 0 meters. For locations south of the equator, the equator is given a false value of 10,000,000 meters and values decrease from north to south.

A UTM coordinate includes the zone, easting coordinate, and northing coordinate; this coordinate describes a specific location using meters (Figure 3-5).

Figure 3-5. UTM coordinate.

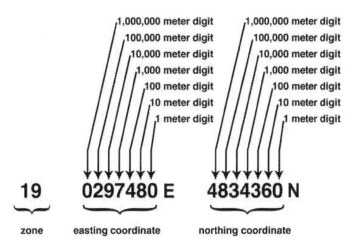

There are different ways that UTM coordinates are written, for example:

- 19 0297480E   4834360N
- 0297480mE   4834360mN
- ²97⁴⁸⁰ᵐE   ⁴⁸34³⁶⁰ᵐN

UTM coordinates are also abbreviated to the extent of accuracy desired; for example, possible abbreviations for UTM 19 0297480E 4834360N include:

UTM Coordinate	Area Covered
297 4834	1000 m by 1000 m square
2974 48343	100 m by 100 m square
29748 483436	10 m by 10 m square
297480 4834360	1 m by 1 m square

Example: This coordinate – 19 0297480E 4834360N – describes a location in New Hampshire.

- The coordinate 0297480E represents an east-west measurement and is the easting. This coordinate is located 202520 meters west of the 19th zone's central meridian line. This number – 202520 meters – was calculated by subtracting the value of 297480 from the false value for the central meridian, which is designated as 500000. The location of this coordinate is 202 thousand, 520 meters west of the 19th zones central meridian line and 4 million, 834 thousand, 360 meters north of the equator.

- The coordinate 4834360N represents a north-south measurement and is the northing. The location of this coordinate is 4,834,360 meters north of the equator in zone 19.

U.S. Public Land Survey

The U.S. Public Land Survey System is another system that is used to describe locations; however, it is not as precise as latitude/longitude or UTM and it is not a global system. It has been used in several states for over 200 years, with only minor modifications. Similar systems are used in parts of Canada, Australia, and a few other areas of the world.

The Public Land Survey System consists of several separate surveys that were used to develop grids for each state. The grid is based on two reference points: a principal meridian running north-south, and a base line running east-west (Figure 3-6). Each grid square represents approximately 36 square miles and is identified as being north or south of a particular base line (township) and east or west of a particular principal meridian (range).

Figure 3-6. Principal meridians and base lines. There are 34 principal meridians and each one has its' own name. Most states on the east coast and Texas (white areas) did not participate in the U.S. Public Land Survey.

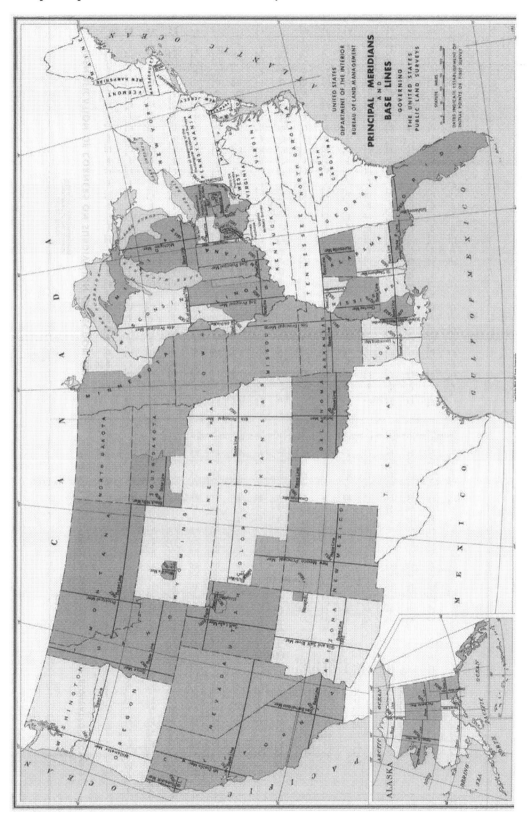

Townships

Township lines, which run east/west and are parallel to the base line, are 6 miles apart (Figure 3-7). Each township is 6 miles square and are numbered based on their location from the principal meridian and base line. For example, the first township line north of the base line is identified as Township 1 North; the second township line north of the base line is identified as Township 2 North, and so on.

The township lines south of the base line are numbered the same (Township 1 South, etc.).

Ranges

Range lines, which run north/south and are parallel to the principal meridian, are 6 miles apart and are numbered much the same as the Township areas (Figure 3-7). For example, the first range line east of the principal meridian is identified as Range 1 East; the second range line east of the principal meridian is identified as Range 2 East, and so on. The range lines west of the principal meridian are numbered the same (Range 1 West, etc.).

Figure 3-7. Example of township and range numbering system.

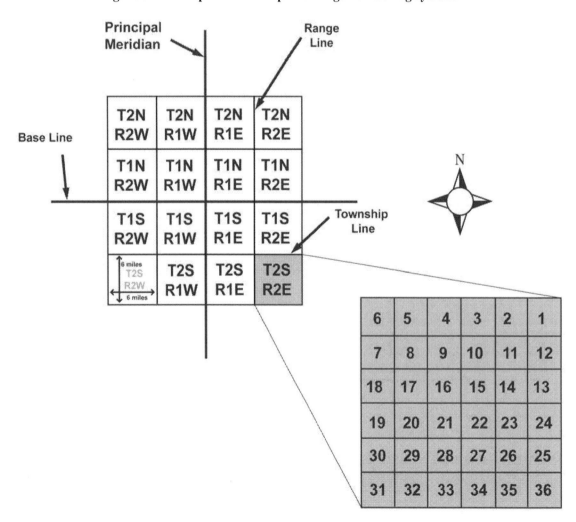

Sections

Within each township are 36 sections, each one mile square. Each section contains 640 acres. The sections are numbered starting in the northeast corner of the township with section 1 and ending in the southeast corner with section 36 (Figure 3-7). If you remember that the northeast corner is always number 1, and that the numbers go sequentially back and forth to the bottom, you will be able to locate section numbers as necessary.

A typical section of 640 acres may be broken down into smaller areas; for example, a half section contains 320 acres, a quarter-section contains 160 acres, half of a quarter contains 80 acres, a quarter of a quarter contains 40 acres, and so on (Figure 3-8). Typically, 2½ acre parcels is the smallest area of a section.

Figure 3-8. This 640 acre section is divided into smaller areas. Areas "A" and "B" in the bottom row represent 2½ acre parcels.

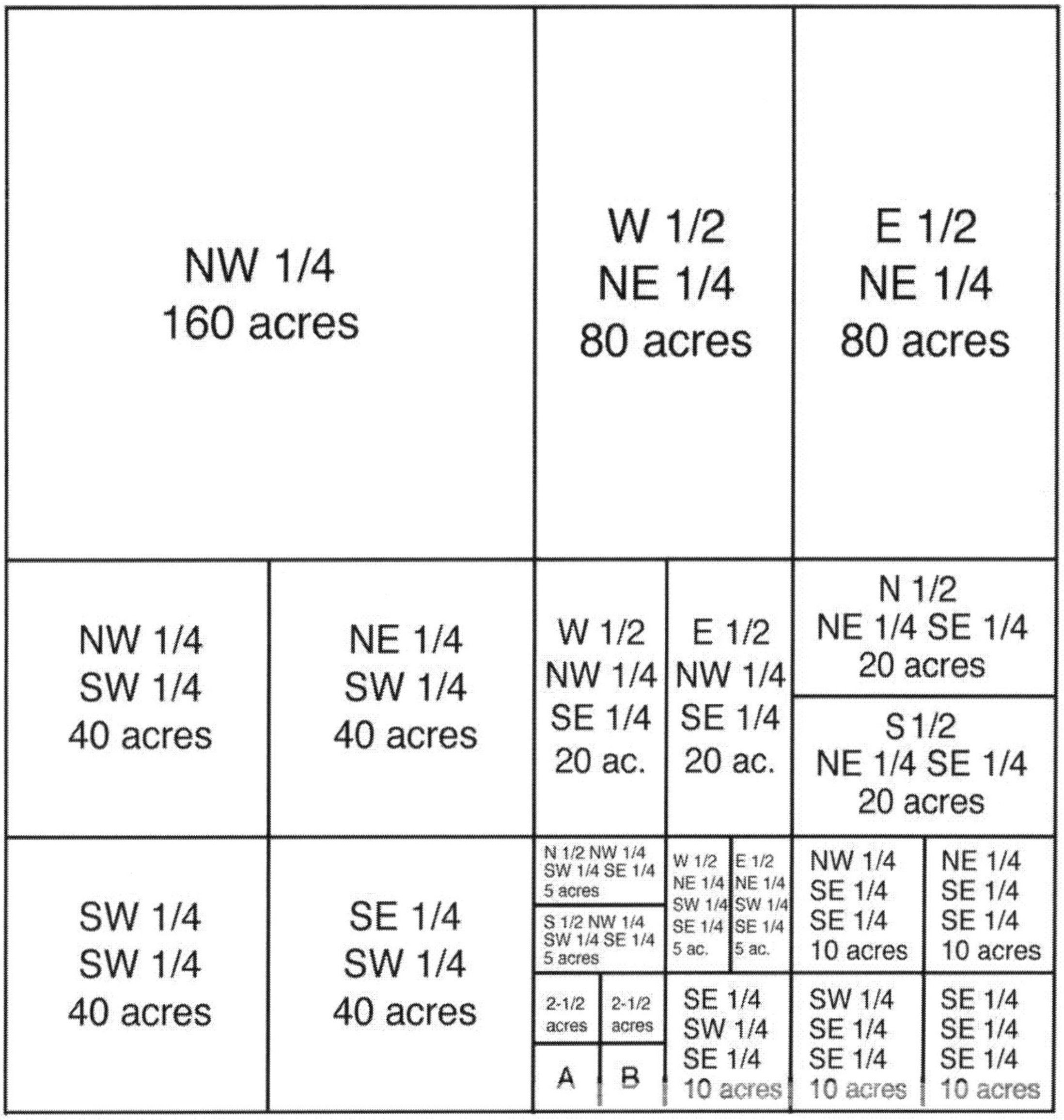

Each area of a section has a unique location description of its own. Below are examples of location descriptions for ½ and ¼ sections within Section 22, Township 5 North, Range 7 West:

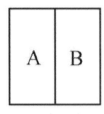

Section 22

Area "A"
W½, Sec. 22, T. 5 N., R. 7 W.

Area "B"
E½, Sec. 22, T. 5 N., R. 7 W.

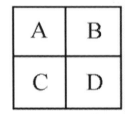

Section 22

Area "C"
N½, Sec. 22, T. 5 N., R. 7 W.

Area "D"
S½, Sec. 22, T. 5 N., R. 7 W.

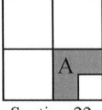

Section 22

Area "A"
NW¼, Sec. 22, T. 5 N., R. 7 W.

Area "B"
NE¼, Sec. 22, T. 5 N., R. 7 W.

Area "C"
SW¼, Sec. 22, T. 5 N., R. 7 W.

Area "D"
SE¼, Sec. 22, T. 5 N., R. 7 W.

Location description for two separate portions of a section (use "and" in the description):

Section 22

Area "A"
N½ and SW¼ SE¼, Sec. 22, T. 5 N., R. 7 W.

Proper descriptions of locations have the section written first followed by the township and range. Descriptions start with the smallest area and end with the largest area. Sometimes, the easiest way to interpret location descriptions is to read them backwards. For example, this is a location description in Leon County, Florida:

SE ¼, Sec.8, T.2N, R.3E, Florida, Tallahassee Meridian
or
Southeast ¼ of section 8, township 2 north and range 3 east, Florida, Tallahassee Meridian

Other Geographic Location Systems

Military Grid Reference System (MGRS)

The Military Grid Reference System is an extension of the UTM system. It is a global reference system used by the U.S. Armed Forces and North Atlantic Treaty Organization (NATO) to locate points on earth. The coordinates are 2 to 10 digits which represent a precision range of 10 kilometers to 1 meter.

Spanish Land Grants

In the southwestern United States, a township frequently will be occupied partially by a Spanish Grant. United States Government Surveys do not cover areas under these grants – the survey stops at the grant boundary. For field references you can just continue known township and range lines into the grant and use the Township/Range description.

Metes and Bounds

Metes and Bounds is a regional system that is a common method of land division in the eastern United States. Metes and bounds is a system of establishing boundaries of tracts of land by reference to natural or artificial monuments along it, as distinguished from those established by beginning at a fixed starting point.

State Land Coordinate Systems

Established in several western states, these systems were developed to measure and record boundary lines, monuments, and other features.

This page intentionally left blank.

Checking Your Understanding

Answers to "Checking Your Understanding" can be found in Appendix B.

1.   What are two common global coordinate systems used in the United States?

2.   Latitude is a measure of how far_____or_____a point is from the_____.

Longitude is a measure of how far_____or_____a point is from the

_____.

3.   On USGS topographic maps, UTM grid lines are marked every_____meters.

4.   This is an abbreviated UTM coordinate: ^{5}66E and ^{51}96N. How else could it be written?

5.   Given this UTM position in Montana – 12 683456E 5346782N – the easting is located

_____meters east of the 12th zone central meridian and the northing is

located_____meters north of the 12th zone equator.

6. Write the acreage and location description (section, township and range) for each of the lettered areas.

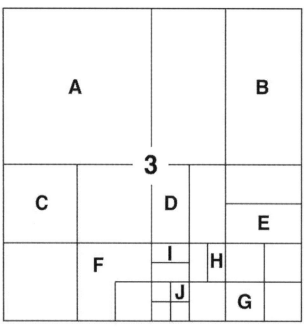

Section 3, Township 2 South, Range 4 E

A. Acres: _____   Location Description: _____

B. Acres: _____   Location Description: _____

C. Acres: _____   Location Description: _____

D. Acres: _____   Location Description: _____

E. Acres: _____   Location Description: _____

F. Acres: _____   Location Description: _____

G. Acres: _____   Location Description: _____

H. Acres: _____   Location Description: _____

I. Acres: _____   Location Description: _____

J. Acres: _____   Location Description: _____

7. Name two other Geographic Location Systems besides latitude/longitude, UTM, and U.S. Public Land Survey.

Chapter 4 – USING A COMPASS AND CLINOMETER

In this chapter you will learn about:

➢ Parts of a compass
➢ Tips on getting accurate compass readings
➢ Adjusting a compass for magnetic declination
➢ Orienting a compass
➢ Taking bearings (direct and back)
➢ Following bearings
➢ Estimating slope with a clinometer

A compass is an instrument that is used for navigation and mapping because it measures the geographic direction between two points. It is a fairly simple instrument that uses a magnet, mounted on a pivot that turns in response to the earth's magnetic field, to determine direction (but not position). The magnetic needle points to the magnetic North Pole, which is different from geographic North Pole. A compass bearing, which is typically expressed as an angle (degrees), refers to the horizontal direction to or from any point. In this publication, the term "bearing" is used interchangeably with the term "azimuth."

A compass is used for several different purposes including:

• Determine direction to a destination or landmark.
• Stay on a straight course to a destination or landmark, even if you lose sight of it.
• Avoid obstacles in the path to the destination or landmark.
• Return to your starting point.
• Pinpoint locations on a map and in the field.
• Identify what you are looking at in the field or on a map.
• Orient a map.
• Plot points on a map.
• Plot route of travel on a map.

There are a variety of different types and models of compasses, such as baseplate, sighting, prismatic, and electronic. This chapter focuses on using a baseplate compass because it is a common, inexpensive, and easy to use compass that does not require batteries.

This chapter starts with discussing the parts of a compass and tips on getting accurate readings. Then it describes adjusting a compass for magnetic declination. Finally it provides step by step instructions on orienting a compass, taking bearings (direct and back bearings), following bearings, and estimating slope with a clinometer.

Refer to Chapter 6, Navigation and Field Mapping, for information on using a compass with a map. Chapter 6 also discusses how to use the compass as a protractor to take a bearing from a map.

Parts of a Compass

The basic parts of a base-plate compass are described below and illustrated in Figure 4-1.

- **Magnetic needle.** The magnetic needle typically has a red end that points to magnetic north, as long as the compass is being used properly and there is no local magnetic attraction.

- **Housing with cardinal points and degrees.** The housing includes a revolving dial that shows the cardinal points (at least north, east, south, and west) and degrees (0 – 360) (Figure 4-2).

- The housing is rotated to line up the compass needle with the orienting arrow when taking a bearing.

- **Orienting arrow.** The north-south orienting arrow (red or black outline of an arrow) is used to align the magnetic needle when taking a bearing. It is also what is adjusted to set the compass for magnetic declination.

- **Orienting lines.** The north-south orienting lines parallel the orienting arrow and can be used to line up the compass dial with grid lines on a map. When the declination is set on a compass with an adjustment screw, the orienting lines no longer parallel the orienting arrow.

- **Index line.** Marked on the front sight of the compass base plate, the index line is where you read the indicated bearing.

- **Direction of travel arrow.** The direction of travel arrow or sighting line is used for sighting and following bearings. The arrow should be pointed in the direction of the destination or landmark.

- **Base plate.** The transparent plate (everything is attached to the baseplate) can be used as a ruler to measure map distances. The direction of travel arrow is also located on the baseplate. Some compasses will have a protractor on the baseplate that can be used to determine bearings from a map.

- **Magnifying lens.** Useful for reading tiny map symbols and features.

- **Declination adjustment screw.** Some compasses have a screw that can be turned to set compass for proper declination. Some compasses have an internal adjustment that automatically corrects for declination.

- **Clinometer.** Some compasses have a clinometer that can be used to estimate slope.

- **Sighting mirror.** Some compasses have a flip up mirror that can improve accuracy when reading bearings. Read the bearing in the dial's reflection where the mirror line crosses it. It can also be used for signaling.

Figure 4-1. Parts of a compass.

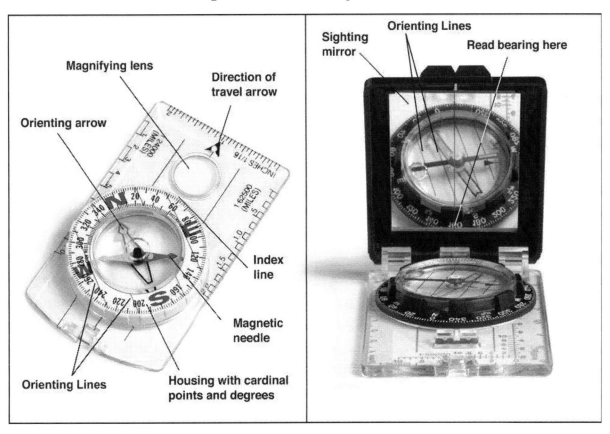

Figure 4-2. Cardinal points and degrees.

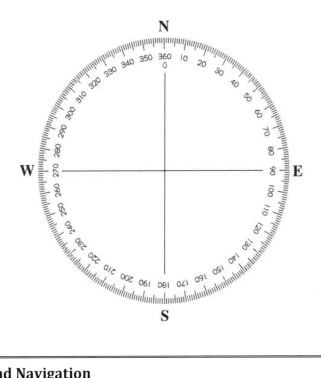

Tips on Getting Accurate Compass Readings

A small error when using a compass can result in a significant error in measurement on the ground. To obtain accurate readings when using a compass:

- Hold the compass level and steady so the needle swings freely.

- Hold the compass about waist high in front of the body, except when using a compass with a sighting mirror or a sighting type compass.

- Raise and lower eyes when taking a bearing, do not move your head. Always use the same eye when taking bearings.

- Directly face object that is being measured.

- Magnetic fields will give incorrect compass readings. Avoid taking readings near magnetic fields such as steel, iron (ferrous metals), vehicles, rebar, and clipboards. Even belt buckles, glasses, and rings can interfere with the compass reading.

- Take bearing twice.

- Adjust for magnetic declination as appropriate.

- Follow the direction of travel arrow, not the compass needle, when walking a bearing. Always follow the line indicated by the compass rather than relying on judgment as to the direction.

- Use back bearings to ensure you are on track when navigating.

Adjusting a Compass for Magnetic Declination

The compass needle always points toward magnetic north; however, topographic maps are drawn in reference to true north (North Pole). The difference between magnetic north and true north is called the angle of magnetic declination, or simply, the declination. Therefore, when using a map and compass together, an adjustment has to be made for declination.

Magnetic declination not only changes with geographic location, but also changes slightly over time. In the contiguous U.S., the magnetic declination generally varies between zero and twenty degrees (Figure 4-3). Only along the zero declination line are true north and magnetic north the same, and therefore, no adjustment has to be made for declination (this is the dark, heavy line labeled as 0° in Figure 4-3).

Figure 4-3. Declination chart of United States.

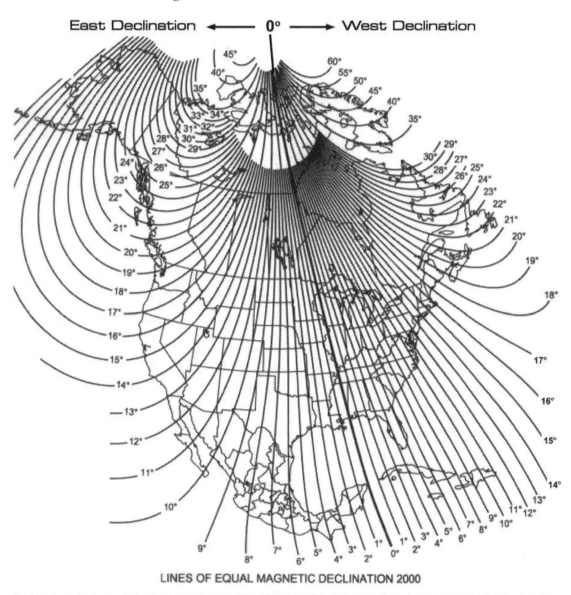

When someone is using their compass in a location that is east of the zero declination line (for example Maine), the needle will point in a direction that is west of true north – this is referred to as westerly declination. When someone is using a compass in a location that is west of the zero declination line (for example Nevada), the needle will point in a direction that is east of true north – this is referred to as easterly declination.

Magnetic Declination on Topographic Maps

Magnetic declination is printed in the lower left hand corner on USGS topographic maps in the arrow diagram or in the information block. Since declination does slightly change over time, topographic maps of the same area can have different declinations if the maps were published on different dates. There are web sites that will provide declination when a zip code is entered.

Adjusting a Compass

Making an adjustment for declination is essential when using a map and compass together. Either the map or the compass needs to be adjusted for declination. It is generally easier to adjust the compass for declination, rather than the map. When the compass is adjusted then geographic north is the reference point for both the compass and the map.

The process for adjusting declination on a compass depends upon the type of compass; therefore, refer to the owner's manual for specific instructions. Some compasses have a declination screw that can be turned which rotates the orienting arrow. Others require the rotation of the center of the case so the orienting arrow is offset by declination. Some compasses are automatically adjusted. It is important to be accurate when setting declination because 1 degree off can result in 920 feet off course in 10 miles.

Orienting a Compass

There are two different ways to orient a compass – to magnetic north or geographic north. The purpose of orienting a compass is so you know your location in relation to north. Orienting a compass to north is also called "boxing the needle" because it refers to aligning the north seeking end of the magnetic needle over the orienting arrow.

Orient to Magnetic North

One method for orienting the compass to magnetic north is described in Table 4-1 and illustrated in Figure 4-4.

Table 4-1. Steps to orient a compass.

Steps	Directions
1	Set 360° or 0° on the compass dial in line with the index line.
2	Hold the base plate and turn your body until the north seeking end of the magnetic needle lines up with the orienting arrow. The direction you are facing is magnetic north.

Figure 4-4. Orient a compass.

Orient to Geographic North

If you are going to use your compass with a map, then orient the compass to geographic north. Adjust the compass for magnetic declination and then follow the steps in Table 4-1.

Taking Bearings (Direct and Back)

Taking a bearing refers to measuring the direction from one point to another, either in the field or on a map. A bearing is the measurement of direction between two points and it is typically expressed as an angle, for example 30 degrees. Bearings taken with a compass that has not been adjusted for magnetic declination are called "magnetic bearings." Whereas bearings taken with a compass that has been adjusted for magnet declination are called "true bearings." This section focuses on taking a direct and back bearing in the field and Chapter 6, Navigation and Field Mapping, addresses how to take a bearing on a map.

Taking a Direct Bearing

A direct bearing is measured from your position towards an object. It tells you the direction from you to the object, destination or landmark. One method for taking a direct bearing is described in Table 4-2 and illustrated in Figure 4-5.

Table 4-2. How to take a direct bearing.

Steps	Directions
1	Adjust compass for declination if using the bearing with a map.
2	Face object and align the direction-of-travel arrow with the object whose bearing you want to measure.
3	Turn the compass housing until the north end of the magnetic needle is aligned with the orienting arrow.
4	Read the bearing where the direction of travel arrow or index line meets the dial. This is the direction to the object, expressed as an angle.

Figure 4-5. Taking a direct bearing.

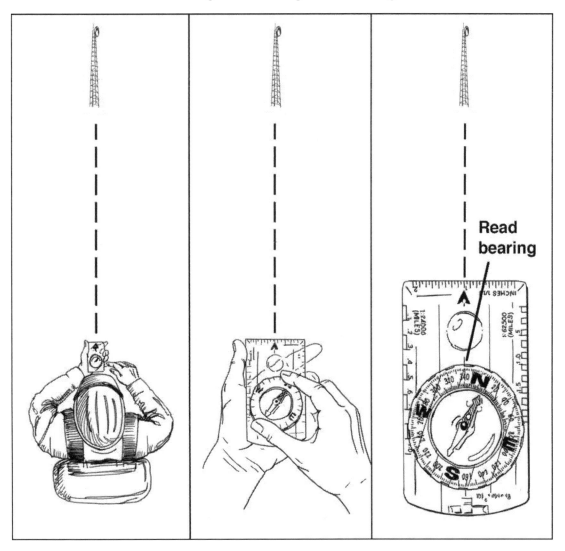

Taking a Back Bearing

A back bearing, which is sometimes called backsighting, is the exact opposite of a bearing – it is measured from the object to your position. The back bearing differs by 180° or the opposite direction from the direct bearing (Figure 4-6).

Figure 4-6. Direct and back bearing.

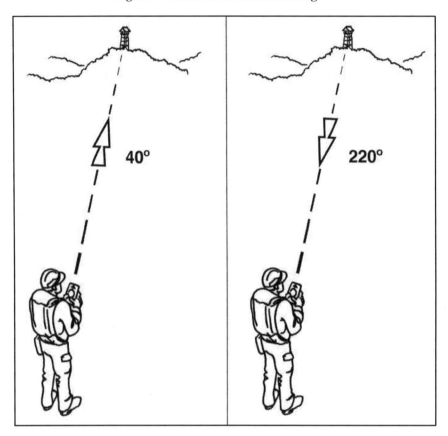

Two common methods for determining a back bearing include:

- Using a compass – similar process to taking a direct bearing, but instead take a back bearing by aligning the south end of the needle with the orienting arrow.

- Using addition and subtraction.

    - If the direct bearing is between zero and 180° **add** 180° to find the back bearing. For example, if the direct bearing is 60° the back bearing is 240°.

    - If the direct bearing is between 180° and 360° **subtract** 180° to find the back bearing.

Back bearings are important because they can be used to communicate your position to someone else, for example, "I am located 145° from the cell tower." They are also used when navigating to help ensure you are on course.

Following Bearings

One of the main reasons for using a compass is to help you follow a straight course to a destination. A bearing can help you stay on course even if you lose sight of your destination due to terrain, vegetation, fog, smoke or other conditions.

Following a bearing refers to setting a bearing on the compass and then following that bearing along a line to the destination. If the final destination is a long distance from starting point or if it is visually obstructed (due to vegetation, terrain, weather, or other condition) look for an intermediate destination (boulder, landmark, identifiable tree) that is on that same bearing. If there are no visible intermediate destinations, another person can serve as the intermediate destination.

One method for following bearings is described in Table 4-3 and illustrated in Figure 4-7.

Table 4-3. How to follow a bearing.

Steps	Directions
1	Adjust compass for declination if using the bearing with a map.
2	Take a bearing of the destination or landmark. If the destination or landmark is a long way away, choose an intermediary object that is visible and located along the line of the direction-of-travel arrow. Don't turn the compass housing after you have taken the bearing.
3	Walk to the intermediary or goal destination by the easiest route, it doesn't have to be straight route. Don't look at your compass while you are walking, just walk towards the destination.
4	Check to make sure you are still aligned with the original bearing. – Stop walking. Hold the compass but don't turn the housing. Turn your body left or right until the north-seeking end of the needle end matches the pointed end of the orienting arrow. The direction-of-travel arrow should now be pointing towards the object. – Take a back bearing to the intermediary or starting point. It should be $180°$ from the direct bearing that was taken from that point. If it isn't – walk to one side or the other until it is. Then turn around and sight ahead on the original bearing. A mistake of a few degrees can result in a significant mistake in distance from your final destination.
5	Repeat steps above until goal object is reached.

Figure 4-7. Following a bearing.

Estimating Slope with a Clinometer

A clinometer is an instrument that measures the angle of a slope. It can also be used to measure elevation or height. There are different types of clinometers and they have different scales. Table 4-4 outlines one method to estimate slope using a clinometer, which is illustrated in Figure 4-8.

Table 4-4. Steps to estimate slope using a clinometer.

Steps	Directions
1	Stand so you are facing directly up or down the slope.
2	Hold clinometer vertically. Keep both eyes open. Use one eye to read the scale inside the hole and the other eye to sight on an object that is about the same height above the ground as your eye level height. Align the horizontal band with this object.
3	Read the appropriate scale in percent or degrees as indicated by the horizontal band.

Figure 4-8. Estimating slope with a clinometer.

Some compasses have a built-in clinometer; however, when using the clinometer on a compass, the slope is reported in degrees, not percent. Figure 4-9 illustrates a general relationship between percent slope and degree slope. Refer to the compass owner's manual for instructions on estimating slope using the built-in clinometer and conversion information.

Figure 4-9. General relationship between percent slope and degree slope.

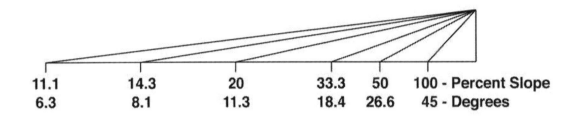

Checking Your Understanding

Answers to "Checking Your Understanding" can be found in Appendix B.

1. List three examples of how you may use a compass on an incident.

2. Label the seven parts of a compass.

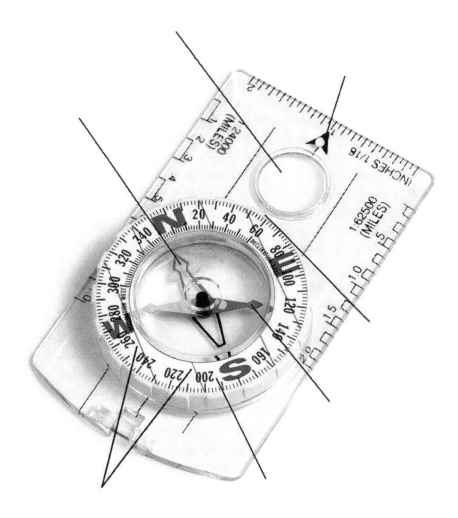

3. List five tips on how to obtain accurate compass readings.

4. How do you adjust your compass for declination? How do you know what the declination is for the area where you are working?

5. What are the two different ways to orient a compass?

6. The following exercises will improve your performance.

   • Practice taking direct bearings and back bearings of various objects.

   • Take a compass bearing of a distant object. Mark your starting location, walk to your object. Now take a back bearing and follow that bearing. How far off were you from your starting point?

   • Practice estimating slope using a clinometer.

Chapter 5 – GLOBAL POSITIONING SYSTEM

In this chapter you will learn about:

➢ How the Global Positioning System works
➢ Using a GPS receiver

The Global Positioning System (GPS) is a satellite based navigation system that can be used to locate positions anywhere on earth. Designed and operated by the U.S. Department of Defense, it consists of satellites, control and monitor stations, and receivers. GPS receivers take information transmitted from the satellites and uses triangulation to calculate a user's exact location. GPS is used on incidents in a variety of ways, such as:

• To determine position locations; for example, you need to radio a helicopter pilot the coordinates of your position location so the pilot can pick you up.

• To navigate from one location to another; for example, you need to travel from a lookout to the fire perimeter.

• To create digitized maps; for example, you are assigned to plot the fire perimeter and hot spots.

• To determine distance between two points or how far you are from another location.

The purpose of this chapter is to give a general overview of the Global Positioning System, not to teach proficiency in the use of a GPS receiver. To become proficient with a specific GPS receiver, study the owner's manual and practice using the receiver. The chapter starts with a general introduction on how the GPS works. Then it discusses some basics on using a GPS receiver.

How the Global Positioning System Works

The basis of the GPS is a constellation of satellites that are continuously orbiting the earth. These satellites, which are equipped with atomic clocks, transmit radio signals that contain their exact location, time, and other information. The radio signals from the satellites, which are monitored and corrected by control stations, are picked up by the GPS receiver. A GPS receiver needs only three satellites to plot a rough, 2D position, which will not be very accurate. Ideally, four or more satellites are needed to plot a 3D position, which is much more accurate.

Three Segments of GPS

The three segments of GPS are the space, control, and user (Figure 5-1).

Figure 5-1. Three segments of GPS.

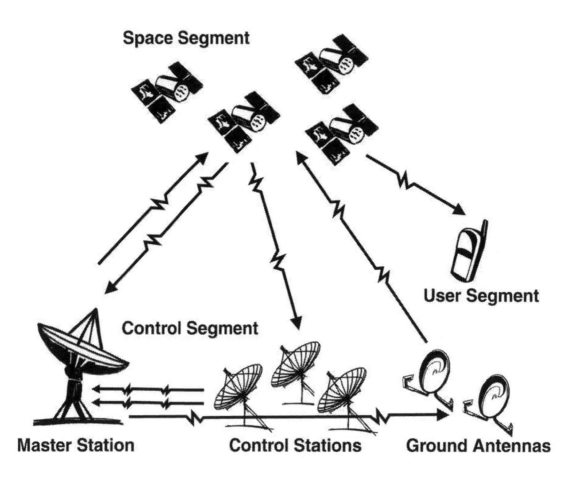

- Space Segment — Satellites orbiting the earth

The space segment consists of 29 satellites circling the earth every 12 hours at 12,000 miles in altitude. This high altitude allows the signals to cover a greater area. The satellites are arranged in their orbits so a GPS receiver on earth can receive a signal from at least four satellites at any given time. Each satellite contains several atomic clocks. The satellites transmit low radio signals with a unique code on different frequencies, allowing the GPS receiver to identify the signals. The main purpose of these coded signals is to allow the GPS receiver to calculate travel time of the radio signal from the satellite to the receiver. The travel time multiplied by the speed of light equals the distance from the satellite to the GPS receiver.

- Control Segment — The control and monitoring stations

The control segment tracks the satellites and then provides them with corrected orbital and time information. The control segment consists of five unmanned monitor stations and one Master Control Station. The five unmanned stations monitor GPS satellite signals and then send that information to the Master Control Station where anomalies are corrected and sent back to the GPS satellites through ground antennas.

- User Segment — The GPS receivers owned by civilians and military

The user segment consists of the users and their GPS receivers. The number of simultaneous users is limitless.

How GPS Determines a Position

The GPS receiver uses the following information to determine a position.

- Precise location of satellites

When a GPS receiver is first turned on, it downloads orbit information from all the satellites called an almanac. This process, the first time, can take as long as 12 minutes; but once this information is downloaded, it is stored in the receiver's memory for future use.

- Distance from each satellite

The GPS receiver calculates the distance from each satellite to the receiver by using the distance formula: distance = velocity x time. The receiver already knows the velocity, which is the speed of a radio wave or 186,000 miles per second (the speed of light). To determine the time part of the formula, the receiver times how long it takes for a signal from the satellite to arrive at the receiver. The GPS receiver multiplies the velocity of the transmitted signal by the time it takes the signal to reach the receiver to determine distance.

- Triangulation to determine position

The receiver determines position by using triangulation. When it receives signals from at least three satellites the receiver should be able to calculate its approximate position (a 2D position). The receiver needs at least four or more satellites to calculate a more accurate 3D position. The position can be reported in latitude/longitude, UTM, or other coordinate system.

Sources of Errors

The GPS is not a perfect system. There are several different types of errors that can occur when using a GPS receiver, for example:

- User mistakes

User mistakes account for most GPS errors; and a GPS receiver has no way to identify and correct these mistakes. Common examples of user mistakes include:

- Inputting incorrect information into a GPS receiver, such as the datum, and when creating a waypoint.

- Unknowingly relying on a 2D position instead of a 3D position for determining position coordinates. This mistake can result in distance errors in excess of a mile. The signal from the satellite may be blocked by buildings, terrain, electronic interference, and sometimes dense foliage. A GPS receiver needs a fairly clear view of the sky to operate.

- The human body can cause signal interference. Holding a GPS receiver close to the body can block some satellite signals and hinder accurate positioning. If a GPS receiver must be hand held without benefit of an external antenna, facing to the south can help to alleviate signal blockage caused by the body because the majority of GPS satellites are oriented more in the earth's southern hemisphere.

- Multipath interference

Multipath interference is caused by the satellite signal reflecting off of vehicles, buildings, power lines, water and other interfering objects (Figure 5-2). Multipath is difficult to detect and sometimes impossible for the user to avoid or for the receiver to correct. When using a GPS receiver in a vehicle place the external antenna on the roof of the vehicle to eliminate most signal interference caused by the vehicle. If the GPS receiver is placed on the dashboard there will always be some multipath interference.

Figure 5-2. Sources of signal interference.

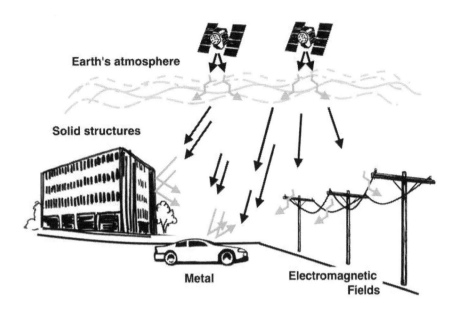

- Satellite and receiver clock errors

These can be slight discrepancies in the satellite's atomic clocks which may cause slight position errors in the GPS receiver. Errors are monitored and corrected by the Master Control Station.

- Orbit errors

Satellite orbit pertains to the altitude, position, and speed of the satellite. Satellite orbits vary due to gravitational pull and solar pressure fluctuations. Orbit errors are also monitored and corrected by the Master Control Station.

- Satellite geometry

The location of GPS satellites in relation to a GPS receiver on the ground can impact the receiver's ability to triangulate a 3D position. The quality of a receiver's triangulated position improves the further apart GPS satellites are located from each other in the sky above the receiver. The quality decreases if the satellites are grouped close together in the sky above the receiver.

- Atmospheric interference

The atmosphere can slow or speed up the satellite signal. Fortunately, error caused by atmospheric conditions (ionized air, humidity, temperature, pressure) has been reduced with the implementation of the Wide Area Augmentation System (WAAS), which is discussed later in this chapter.

- SelectiveAvailability

  SelectiveAvailability is the intentional degradation (limits accuracy of satellite signals) of the GPS system by the U.S. Department of Defense for security reasons. At this time there is no Selective Availability in force; however, it can be reactivated without notice to GPS users.

- Correction systems

  Correction systems have been designed to reduce some of the sources of error with GPS.

- Real-time Differential GPS

  Real-time Differential GPS (DGPS) employs a second, stationary GPS receiver at a precisely measured spot, usually established through traditional survey methods (Figure 5-3). This receiver corrects or reduces errors found in the GPS signals, including atmospheric distortion, orbital anomalies, Selective Availability (when it existed), and other errors. A DGPS station is able to do this because its computer already knows its precise location, and can easily determine the amount of error provided by the GPS signals. DGPS cannot correct for GPS receiver noise in the user's receiver, multipath interference, and user mistakes. In order for DGPS to work properly, both the user's receiver and the DGPS station receiver must be accessing the same satellite signals at the same time.

Figure 5-3. Real-Time Differential GPS.

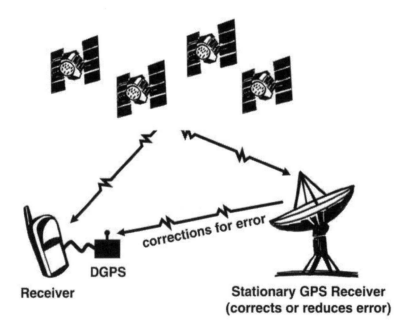

- Wide Area Augmentation System

  The Wide Area Augmentation System (WAAS) is an experimental system designed to enhance and improve aircraft flight approaches using GPS and WAAS satellites. The WAAS can be considered an advanced real-time differential GPS. It uses its own geo-stationary satellites positioned over the equator to transmit corrected GPS signals to receivers capable of receiving these signals.

  Problems with WAAS include poor signal reception under dense tree canopy and in canyons, as well as decreased capability in northerly latitudes. Many GPS receivers are now capable of receiving the WAAS signal. However, WAAS should not be considered a consistently reliable source for improving the accuracy of GPS until the technology improves.

Using a GPS Receiver

There are several different models and types of GPS receivers. Refer to the owner's manual for your GPS receiver and practice using it to become proficient.

When working on an incident with a GPS receiver it is important to:

- Always have a compass and a map.

- Have a GPS download cable.

- Have extra batteries.

- Know memory capacity of the GPS receiver to prevent loss of data, decrease in accuracy of data, or other problems.

- Use an external antennae whenever possible, especially under tree canopy, in canyons, or while flying or driving.

- Set up GPS receiver according to incident or agency standard regulation; coordinate system.

- Take notes that describe what you are saving in the receiver.

Inputs

Each time you use a GPS receiver, you will need to input information such as:

- Position format units (example: UTM 11T 0557442m E 4836621m N).

  This input determines the way positions are displayed on the receiver screen. For example, sometimes you may want to use latitude/longitude coordinates and other times it may be better to use UTM coordinates.

- Map datum (example: WGS 84, NAD 27 and NAD 83).

  This input ensures that your GPS receiver and map are both using the same datum, which is extremely important for accuracy.

- Distance units (feet, miles, meters).

- Elevation units (feet or meters).

- North reference (true, magnetic, or grid).

- Time format (12 or 24 hour) and time zone.

Waypoints

A waypoint is a position based on geographic coordinate values, such as latitude/longitude and UTM, stored in the GPS receiver's memory. They are sometimes referred to as landmarks. Once the waypoint is saved it remains static in the GPS receiver's memory until edited or deleted.

How Waypoints are Determined

A waypoint can either be a saved position fix or can be created by manually entering coordinates into the receiver.

- To turn a position location into a waypoint is simply a matter of saving the receiver's current position as a waypoint. The receiver will give the position coordinates an alpha-numeric name or the user can designate a name. Once a position fix is saved, it becomes a waypoint with static coordinates saved in the receiver's memory.

- Users can enter waypoints into the GPS receiver. For example, coordinates on a map or coordinates radioed in from a remote location can be entered into a GPS receiver.

Naming Waypoints

The GPS receiver will automatically name waypoints with an alpha-numeric name; however, it is best if you designate a unique name for each waypoint so you will know exactly what the waypoint is referring to. Use short descriptive designations because long names can be hard to read when they are downloaded. You can make up your own names as long as you know what they are. Some possible designations include:

- D1, D2, D3 for different dozer lines
- HL1, HL2, HL3 for different hand lines
- DP1, DP2, DP3 for different drop points
- H1, H2, H3 for different helispots
- A1, A2, A3 for different access points

Record a description of each waypoint in your notes otherwise it will be difficult to remember.

Routes

Routes are just a sequence of waypoints (Figure 5-4). When navigating a route, the GPS receiver will automatically change the destination waypoint to the next waypoint on the list as it reaches each waypoint.

Once one waypoint is passed, the GPS receiver will navigate to the next waypoint. When a route is first activated, the GPS receiver will assume that the first leg is A to B. B is the waypoint being navigated to and A is the anchor point that defines the first leg of the route.

Figure 5-4. Example of a "route" that is displayed on a GPS receiver screen.

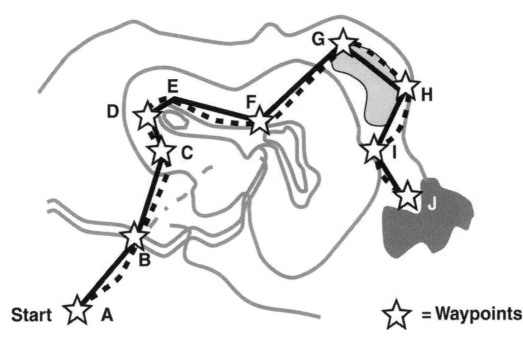

Terminology

There is a lot of terminology associated with using a GPS receiver. Some of the common terms are defined below and illustrated in Figure 5-5.

Figure 5-5. GPS navigation terminology.

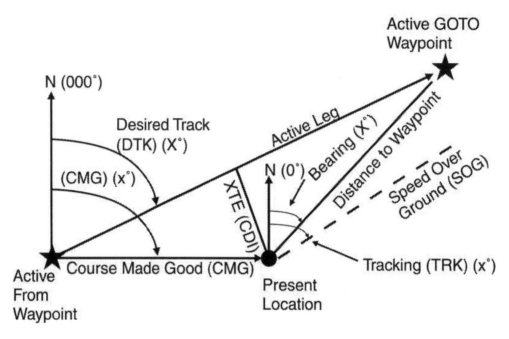

- Active from Waypoint
- This is the starting waypoint or the receiver's last waypoint in an active route.
- Active GOTO Waypoint
- This is the designated destination in the receiver, whether in an active route or as a single waypoint.
- Active Leg

Active leg is always a straight line between the last waypoint and the GOTO waypoint. A GPS receiver always plots the most efficient, straight-line course of travel between two points – the active leg. If the receiver is following a route, the active leg will be the desired track between the last waypoint in the route, and the next waypoint in the route. If the receiver has deviated from the route, the receiver selects the closest leg to its position and makes it the active leg in the route (the next waypoint in the route list becomes the GOTO destination waypoint).

- Bearing (BRG)/Desired Track (DTK)

  In GPS the term bearing is used instead of azimuth. As used in GPS, bearing is the compass direction (expressed in degrees) from the present position to desired destination waypoint or the compass direction between any two waypoints.

- Course Deviation Indicator (CDI)

  This graphically shows the amount and direction of Crosstrack Error.

- Course Made Good (CMG) or Course Over Ground (COG)

  This is the present direction of travel expressed in degrees from north. It is not necessarily the most direct path.

- Crosstrack Error (XTE)

  This is the distance off the desired track (active leg) on either side of the active leg. It's the linear difference between the Desired Track (DTK) and your actual Course Made Good (CMG).

- Desired Track (DTK)

  This is a function of GOTO. It is shown in degrees from north. DTK is measured along the active leg (a straight line between two waypoints in a route) or from your current position to a designated GOTO waypoint, when not navigating a route.

- Estimated Position Error (EPE)

  A measurement of horizontal position error in feet or meters based upon a variety of factors including dilution of precision (DOP) and satellite signal quality.

- Estimated Time En Route (ETE)

  The time left to destination based upon present speed and course.

- Estimated Time of Arrival (ETA)

  The time of day of arrival at a destination

- Fix

  A single position with latitude, longitude (or grid position), altitude, time, and date.

- GOTO Function

  The GOTO function gives GPS receivers the capability of leading a person to any specified place. Simply enter the coordinate of desired destination into the GPS receiver as a waypoint and then, by using the GOTO function, tell the receiver to guide to destination. The receiver guides to destination using a steering screen. There are several different versions of a steering screen, but they all point in the direction needed to travel to from present position to the waypoint selected.

- GOTO Waypoint

  If traveling from one waypoint to another (using GOTO), then XTE will show the distance of deviation of your actual route from the active leg (a straight line) between those waypoints.

- Speed Over Ground (SOG)

  This is the velocity you are traveling.

- Tracking (TRK)/ Heading (HDG)

  This is the direction you are actually traveling or heading, expressed in degrees from north.

- Track Log

  A track log is the GPS unit's record of travel or where you have been. As you move along, your every movement is being stored. Receivers with a TracBack feature will allow you to reverse your route taking you back the same way you originally traveled. As you move along, most GPS receivers show your track on a map screen.

- Velocity Made Good (VMG)

  Velocity made good is the speed at which the destination is approached. If you are directly on course, VMG is the same value as SOG, but if you stray from course, VMG decreases and is less than SOG.

Checking Your Understanding

Answers to "Checking Your Understanding" can be found in Appendix B.

1. Practice storing and naming waypoints and tracks using a GPS receiver.

2. Determine how many waypoints your GPS receiver can store in the memory.

3. List three ways you can prevent making user mistakes when using a GPS receiver.

4. List three things that are important to do when you are taking a GPS receiver with you on an incident.

5. How should you name waypoints?

This page intentionally left blank.

Chapter 6 – NAVIGATION AND FIELD MAPPING

In this chapter you will learn about:

➤ Orienting maps
➤ Measuring a bearing on a map
➤ Plotting points on a map using latitude/longitude
➤ Plotting points on a map using UTM
➤ Estimating your own position location
➤ Estimating unknown position locations
➤ Estimating distance on the ground
➤ Field mapping
➤ Taking notes

Navigation and field mapping skills will help you know where you are, where you are going, how you are going to get there, how long it will take, and when you will get back. Even in rough terrain and poor visibility these skills can help you get to your destination by choosing the best route with the least resistance. Always have a compass and map when navigating, do not rely only on a GPS receiver. Field mapping is also important because operational decisions are made based on the information on the field maps.

This chapter builds on what you learned in all the other chapters. It starts with how to orient a map. Then it outlines the steps on how to measure a bearing on a map, plot points using latitude/longitude and UTM coordinates, estimate your own position location, and estimate unknown position locations. Next it discusses the different methods for estimating distance on the ground, such as pacing. Finally, it addresses field mapping and note taking.

To complete the "Checking Your Understanding" section in this chapter you will need the following tools:

• Compass
• Protractor
• Engineer's 20 scale ruler
• UTM grid reader

Appendix C, Tools and Resources, has a copy of a protractor, engineer's 20 scale ruler, and UTM grid reader that can be photocopied on a clear plastic sheet. After photocopying, check to make sure the scale has not changed.

The methods described in this chapter are based on geographic north (not magnetic north) being the point of reference. In other words, the compass is adjusted for declination not the map.

Orienting Maps

Orienting the map to true north is key to navigating successfully. Orienting a map also gives you a general idea of your own location on the map. This section describes two methods to orient a map: topographical orientation and compass orientation.

Orienting a Map with Topographical Features

Table 6-1 describes how to orient a map with topographic features and is illustrated in Figure 6-1.

Table 6-1. Steps to orient a map using topographical features.

Steps	Directions
1	Find your approximate location on the map.
2	Select two prominent topographical features or landmarks that are visible to you and shown on the map.
3	Turn the map until the features on the map are in proper relation to the actual features in the field. The map is now oriented.

Figure 6-1. Orient a map using topographical features.

Chapter 6 – Basic Land Navigation

Orienting a Map with a Compass

If there are limited topographical features for orienting a map, then orient the map with a compass. However, adjust the compass for declination before using it with a map. One method for orienting a map with a compass is described in Table 6-2 and illustrated in Figure 6-2.

Table 6-2. Steps to orient a map using a compass.

Steps	Directions
1	Adjust compass for declination as appropriate. Make sure there is no local magnetic attraction.
2	Rotate the compass housing so north or 360° is at the index line or direction of travel line on the compass.
3	Place one side of the compass base plate along the right or left hand edge of the map. The direction-of-travel line must be toward the top of the map.
4	Carefully rotate the map and compass together until the needle is aligned with orienting arrow. The map and compass are now oriented.

Figure 6-2. Orienting a map with compass.

Measuring a Bearing on a Map

The main reason for measuring a bearing on a map is to help with navigation, for example:

- You know where you are on the map and you want to go towards the Incident Command Post (ICP), which is on the map, but it is several miles away over hilly terrain.

- You know where you are on the map and you want to go to a higher elevation for a better view of a potential safety zone, but you can't get there directly because of a wetland.

- You know where you are on the map and you want to go to the lookout, but you can't see it because of morning fog.

A protractor or compass can be used to measure a map bearing; a protractor is easier to use and more accurate than a compass. There are different types of protractors, but a common one is made out of flat clear plastic and is in the shape of a semi-circle with degree marks.

Using a Protractor to Measure a Bearing on a Map

Table 6-3 describes one method of how to measure a bearing using a protractor and is illustrated in Figure 6-3.

Table 6-3. Steps to measure a bearing on a map using a protractor.

Steps	Directions
1	Center the protractor over the starting point and orient 0° with true north (the 0° line needs to be parallel to edge of map).
2	Draw a line on the map from the starting point towards the destination. If you don't want to draw a line on your map align a string or ruler with the start point and destination point.
3	Read the bearing where the line, string or ruler intersects the protractor. This is the direction of travel to your destination.
4	Before using this bearing in the field, adjust the compass for declination.

Figure 6-3. Measuring a bearing with a protractor.

Using a Compass to Measure a Bearing on a Map

A compass can also be used to measure a bearing on a map. One way to measure a magnetic bearing is described in Table 6-4 and illustrated in Figure 6-4. Table 6-5 describes one way to measure a true bearing.

Table 6-4. Steps to measuring a magnetic bearing on a map using a compass.

Steps	Directions
1	Adjust compass for map declination. Disregard the magnetic needle.
2	Place the compass on the map, where one edge of the base plate touches both the start point and destination point. The direction of travel arrow needs to point towards the direction of the destination.
3	Turn the compass housing so that the meridian lines are parallel to map edge and longitude lines.
4	Read bearing at the index line. This is the direction in degrees of the magnetic bearing.

Figure 6-4. Measuring a bearing with a compass where the edge of the base plate touches both the start point (unimproved road) and destination point (lake that is east of spillway elevation 3008 point).

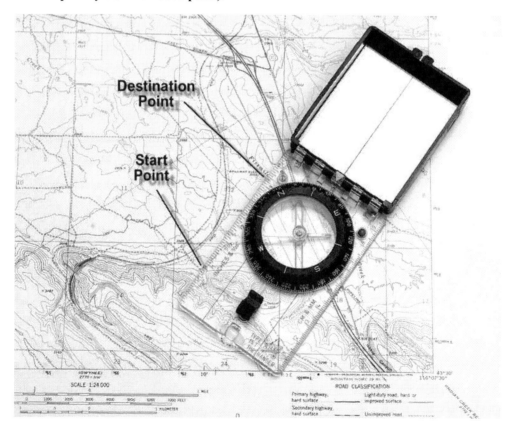

Table 6-5. Steps to measuring a true bearing on a map using a compass.

Steps	Directions
1	Set compass at 0° declination. Disregard the magnetic needle.
2	Place the compass on the map, where one edge of the base plate touches both the start point and destination point. The direction of travel arrow needs to point towards the direction of the destination.
3	Turn the compass housing so that the orienting arrow points to true north, parallel to map edge and longitude lines.
4	Read the true bearing at the index line.

Plotting Points on a Map using Latitude/Longitude

There are many ways to plot points on a map using latitude/longitude; this section describes one method. The grid system of intersecting lines that is used in the latitude/longitude coordinate system makes it easier to plot a point. Once you know how to plot points you can use the same method to determine the coordinates of a point. Examples of when you may need to plot a point on a map or determine the coordinates of a point include:

- To map the location of a safety hazard that is near the fire perimeter.
- To communicate the location of a potential drop site or water source.
- To map the location of a hot spot.
- To assist with navigation.

When working with latitude/longitude coordinates, it is very important to clearly communicate (verbally or written) the coordinates to other incident personnel. It is extremely easy to say the wrong latitude or longitude.

The method described in this section is used only for points located in the northern hemisphere; if the point is in the southern hemisphere there is a different process.

Rulers

Two types of rulers, engineer's ruler and latitude/longitude ruler, are often used to measure latitude and longitude of a point or to plot coordinates. Graduation marks on the ruler may be in seconds, tenths of a minute, or other unit. With either type of ruler, latitude needs to be measured with the ruler oriented north and south; whereas for measuring longitude the ruler needs to be placed diagonally (since the distance between longitude lines is not constant).

- The **engineer's ruler** or scale needs to have 20 graduations per inch. The primary function of the engineer's ruler is to measure distance: 1 inch equals 2000 feet on a 1:24,000 scale topographic map. An engineer's ruler or scale, with 20 graduations per inch (Figure 6-5), can be used for measuring latitude/longitude on a 1:24,000 scale topographic map where each graduation is equal to 1 second.

Figure 6-5. Engineer's 20 scale ruler (not to scale).

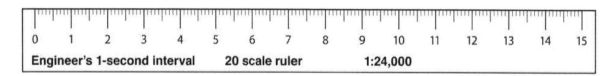

- The **latitude/longitude ruler** usually has minutes and seconds on one edge and decimal minutes on the other edge (Figure 6-6). These rulers are specifically made for different map scales and they come in different increments. Make sure the scale on the ruler matches the map scale.

Figure 6-6. Latitude/longitude ruler (not to scale).

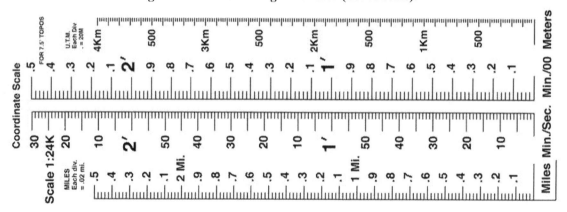

Plotting Latitude and Longitude

When plotting latitude/longitude, it may be helpful to draw the latitude/longitude lines on the map as illustrated in Figure 6-7. You can use these lines as a reference when plotting points.

Figure 6-7. Draw the latitude/longitude lines on the map for reference when plotting points.

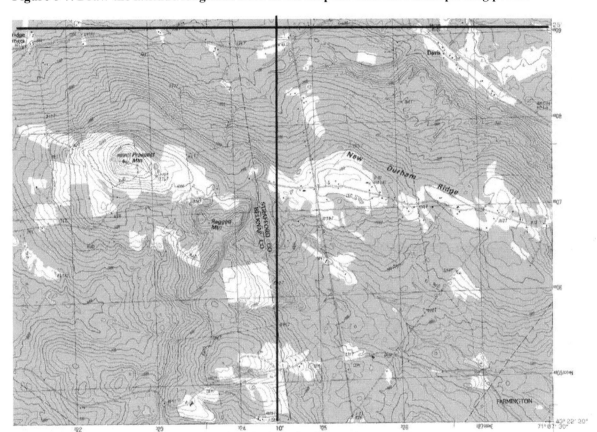

Tables 6-6 and 6-7 illustrate the steps for plotting the coordinate 43°-23'-45" latitude and 71°-08'-36" longitude. An engineer's ruler (each graduation equals one second) is used in the illustrations.

Table 6-6. Steps for plotting the latitude coordinate 43°-23'-45"

Step	Directions
1	On the map below, find the latitude lines that are identified with tick marks.

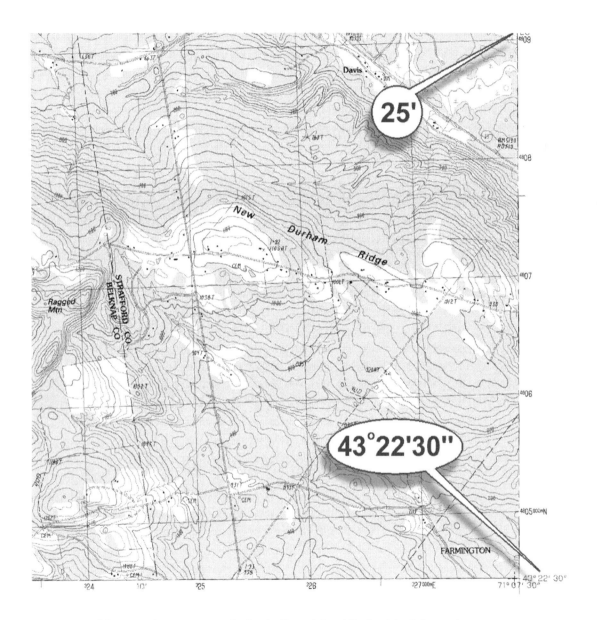

On this map there are two latitude lines identified with tick marks.

Step	Directions
2	Identify the first latitude line that is south of the given latitude coordinate. Determine how many minutes and/or seconds the southern latitude line is from the given latitude coordinate. To do this, subtract the southern latitude line coordinate from the given coordinate: 43° 23' 45" (given coordinate) − 43° 22' 30" (southern latitude line coordinate) 1' 15" or 75" (difference) The resulting number of minutes and/or seconds is referred to as the "difference" and will be used in step 3.

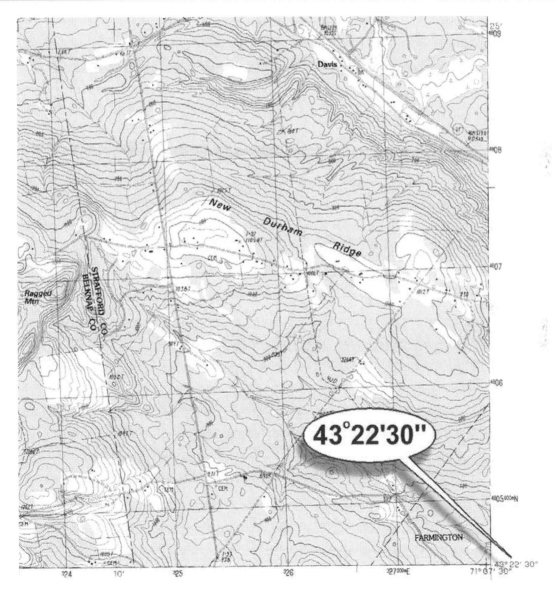

The first latitude line south of the given latitude coordinate is 43° 22' 30".

It is 1'15" or 75" from the given coordinate.

Step	Directions
3	Verify that the scale on the ruler matches the map scale. When measuring latitude orient the ruler north to south. On the right side of the map, place the ruler with the "0" on the southern latitude line. Then, measure the "difference" (as determined in step 2) on the ruler and mark this point. Repeat this on the other side of the map.

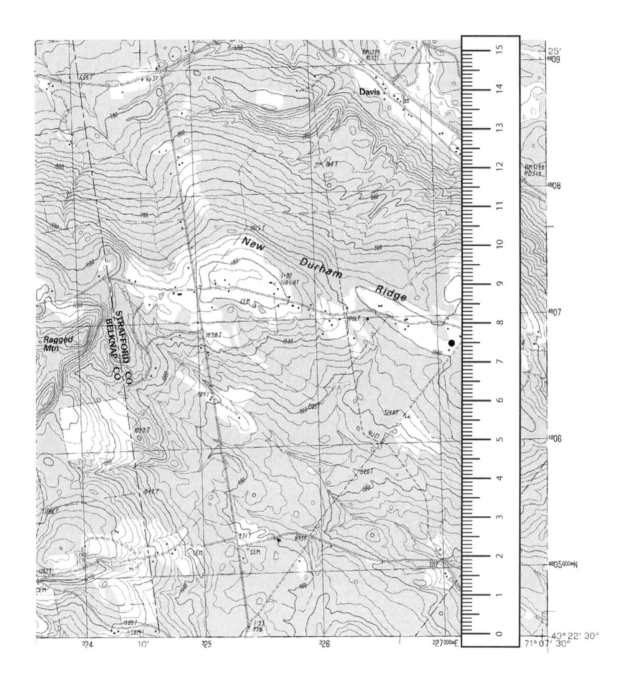

Measure the difference (1'15" or 75") on the ruler and plot the point.

Step	Directions
4	Draw a line connecting the two points.

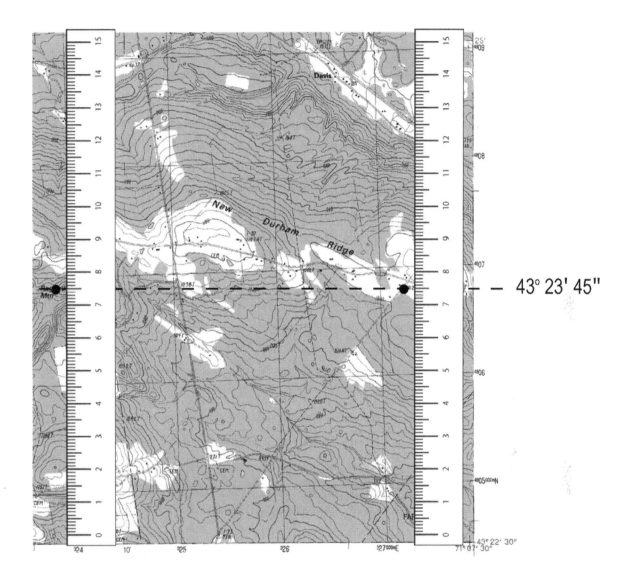

43° 23' 45"

The latitude coordinate 43° 23' 45" is marked with the dashed line.

Table 6-7. Steps for plotting the longitude coordinate 71°-08'-36"

Step	Directions
1	On the bottom of the map, find the longitude lines that are identified with tick marks.

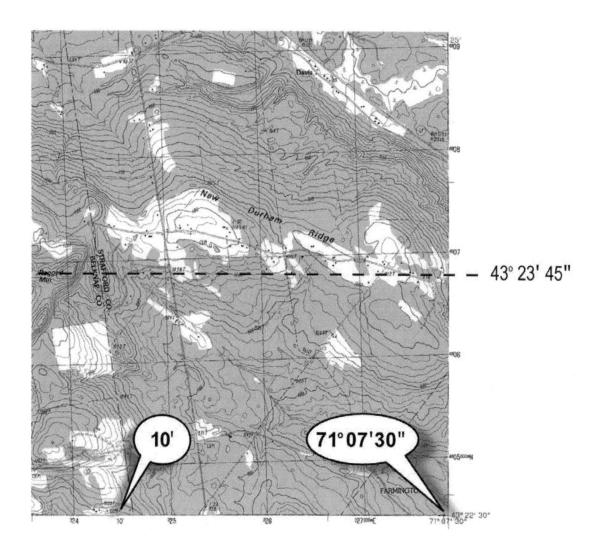

On this map there are two longitude lines identified with tick marks.

Step	Directions
2	Identify the first longitude line that is **east** of the given longitude coordinate and the first longitude line that is **west** of the given longitude coordinate. Draw these lines on the map because they will be used as a reference in step 3. Determine how many minutes and/or seconds the eastern longitude line is from the given longitude coordinate. To do this, subtract the eastern longitude line coordinate from the given coordinate: 71° 08' 36" (given coordinate) – 71° 07' 30" (eastern longitude line coordinate) 1' 6" or 66" (difference) The resulting number of minutes and/or seconds is referred to as the "difference" and will be used in step 3.

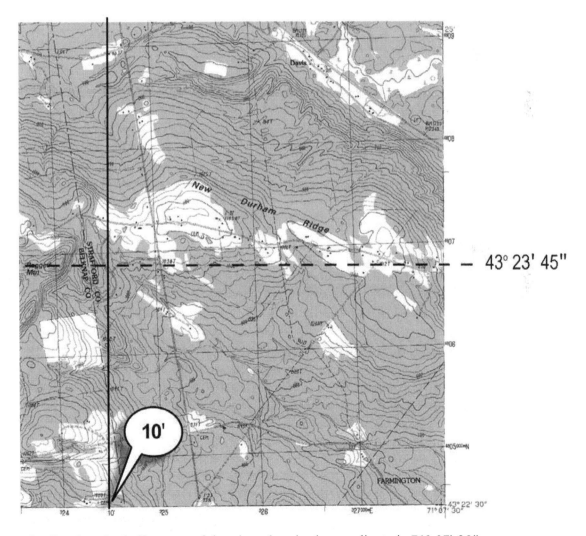

The first longitude line east of the given longitude coordinate is 71°-07'-30".
The first longitude line west of the given longitude coordinate is 71°-10'-00".

Steps	Directions
3	Verify that the scale on the ruler matches the map scale. When measuring longitude orient the ruler on a diagonal. Using the engineer's ruler, place the "0" on the eastern longitude line and place the "15" (150 seconds) on the western longitude line that is 2.5 minutes (150 seconds) from the eastern line. Slide the ruler vertically (keeping the "0" and the "15" graduation marks on their respective longitude line) until the "difference" (as measured on the ruler) lines up with the previously drawn latitude line. Mark this point – it represents the latitude and longitude coordinate.

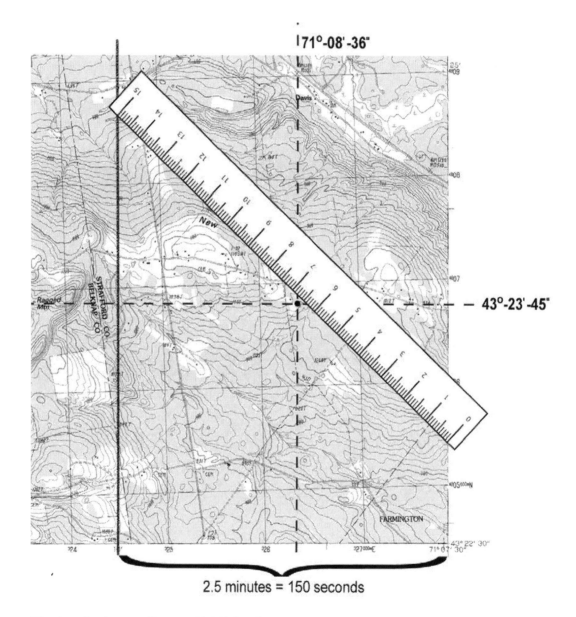

2.5 minutes = 150 seconds

The longitude coordinate 71°-08'-36" is 1' 6" or 66" from the eastern longitude line.
The point represents the coordinate: 43°-23'-45"   71°-08'-36"

Plotting Points on a Map using UTM

When working with UTM coordinates it is essential to have a UTM grid reader. There are many different types of UTM readers and they all work differently; one example is illustrated in Figure 6-8. A grid reader is usually printed on a transparent plastic sheet. Appendix C has a grid reader that you can photocopy on a transparent plastic sheet. When using a grid reader to plot points on a map, the scale on the grid reader must match the scale of the map.

Figure 6-8. This is a UTM grid reader for 1:24,000 map scale (not to scale). The "1" represents 100 meters, "2" represents 200 meters, and so on. The numbers on the right are used to determine the northing coordinate location and the numbers on the top are used to determine the northing coordinate location and the numbers on the top are used to determine the casting coordinate location. The point is plotted in the right corner.

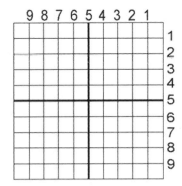

1:24,000 UTM Grid
Each mark is 100 meters

Table 6-8 illustrates the steps for plotting the UTM coordinates 0297480E and 4834360N.

Table 6-8. Steps for plotting UTM coordiantes.

Steps	Directions
1	Find the northing and easting tick marks on the map. Identify the UTM grid square in which the given coordinate is located.

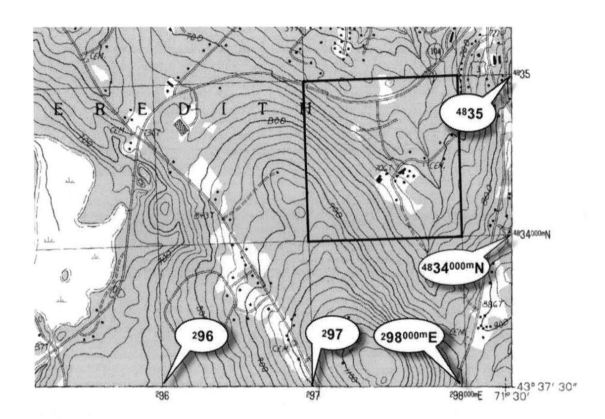

Chapter 6 – Basic Land Navigation

Steps	Directions
2	Place the right corner of the grid reader in this grid square, and • Slide the grid reader so that the last three numbers of the easting coordinate (480) align on the north-south UTM coordinate (0297), then • Slide the grid reader so that the last three numbers of the northing coordinate (360) align on the east-west UTM coordinate (4834).

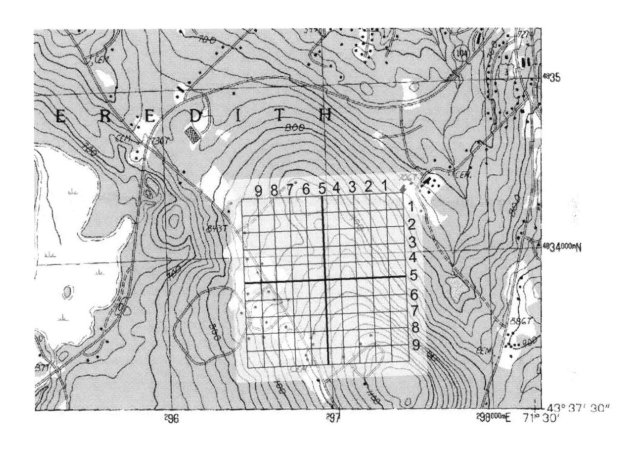

Steps	Directions
3	Plot point of UTM coordinate in upper right corner of grid reader.

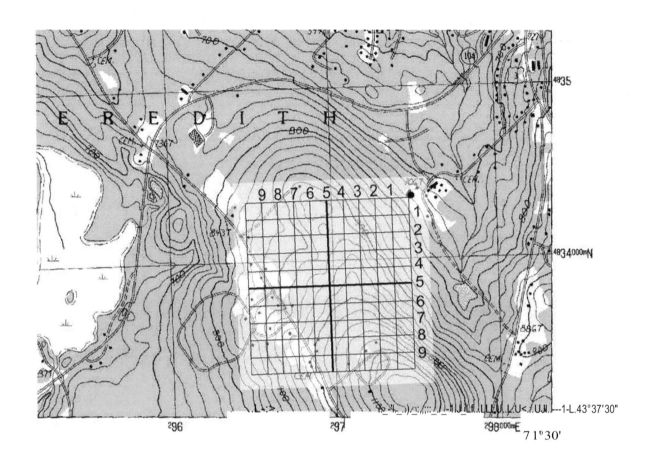

Chapter 6 – Basic Land Navigation

Estimating Your Own Position Location

There may be times in the field when you do not know where you are on the map or you may need to communicate your position location to the Operations Section or Situation Unit. One method to estimate your own position is called triangulation. It involves sighting on two known landmarks (you know where they are on the map) and where those lines of position intersect is where your position is located. Table 6-9 outlines one method to determine your own position using triangulation and is illustrated in Figure 6-9.

Table 6-9. Steps to determine your own position using triangulation.

Steps	Directions
1	Adjust compass for declination.
2	Locate two or more objects (e.g., topographic features, structures), that can be identified on the map. It is best if the objects are approximately 90° apart to reduce potential errors.
3	Take a bearing to each of the objects.
4	Convert to back bearings.
5	On the map, draw the lines of the back bearing from the objects – these are called lines of position. The point where these lines intersect is your position.

Figure 6-9. Estimate your own position by taking bearings and drawing lines of position on a map; where they intersect is your position location.

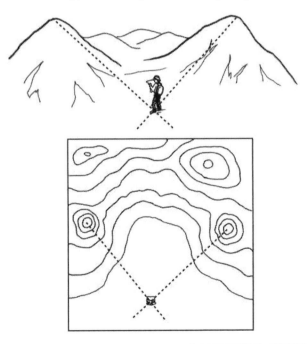

Estimating Unknown Position Locations

Triangulation is also used to estimate the location of an unknown position. For example, two field observers spot smoke. The field observers know their own position locations but they don't know the position of the smoke. They can determine the location of the smoke by taking a bearing and plotting it on the map. The intersection of the two lines is the location of the smoke. Table 6-10 outlines one method for estimating unknown positions and is illustrated in Figure 6-10.

Table 6-10. Steps to estimate an unknown position.

Steps	Directions
1	Adjust compass for declination.
2	Take a bearing from two or more **known** locations to the **unknown** position.
3	Plot bearings on the map and draw connecting lines. The point where the lines insect is the approximate location of the previously unknown position.

Figure 6-10. Estimating an unknown position.

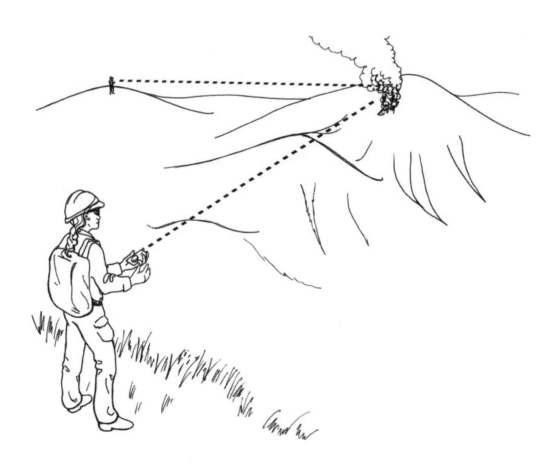

Estimating Distance on the Ground

Being able to estimate distance on the ground is important for both navigation and field mapping. Maps measure the distance between two points "as the crow flies." This means they measure horizontal distances, not slope distances (Figure 6-11). When navigating, if the land is flat this causes no problems, but when there are hills and mountains, distances measured on maps are going to be way off.

Figure 6-11. Map distances can under-estimate the actual ground distance.

470 ft. total ground distance

384 ft. flat map distance

There are various methods of determining distance along the ground. Since it is not usually practical to measure long distances on uneven terrain with a measuring tape, other methods such as pacing must be used. This section focuses on estimating distance using pacing and briefly mentions other methods for estimating distance on the ground.

Pacing

Pacing is one way to keep track of your distance when in the field. A pace is defined as the average length of two natural steps (a count is made each time the same foot touches the ground). Everyone has a different pace. Estimate your own average length of a pace by following the steps in Table 6-11.

Table 6-11. Steps to determine your own pace.

Steps	Directions
1	Set up three pacing courses to ensure an accurate determination of pace length. Each course needs to be 100' or 66' (one chain). One course needs to be on level ground and the other two need to be on a moderate slope and steep slope.
2	Walk each course and count the number of paces (each double-step).
3	Calculate your pace by dividing the distance measured (100' or 66') by average number of paces.
4	Repeat this process a number of times to get your average pace.

To estimate the distance between two points on the ground, count the number of paces as you walk between the two points. Then multiply the number of paces by the length of your average pace. It is a good idea to have a system to record your pace count, especially over long distances.

- Pacing is not exact and one has to compensate for the following:

- Pace can change based on steepness of slope; typically, pace lengthens down slope and shortens upslope.

- Walking into strong winds causes the pace to shorten; walking with a tail wind causes it to lengthen.

- Soft surfaces such as sand and gravel tend to shorten the pace.

- In wet, rainy, or icy conditions, the pace tends to shorten.

- A paced distance may vary from a map distance because land surveys are based on horizontal distances, not slope distances, especially in uneven or rough topography.

Other Methods to Estimate Distance

There are other methods to estimate distance such as using your vehicle odometer and visual comparison. The odometer works great if you need to measure distances where roads are located. Occasionally you will encounter a stream too deep to wade or a slope too steep to cross, and the distance must be estimated. One way to do this is visually compare it to a known distance, such as the length of a football field.

Field Mapping

Field maps are usually drawn on topographic maps but they can also be drawn on other types of maps or on plain paper. Ideally, you will have a standard USGS topographic map with the margins and scales; however, there will be times when you have just a portion of a map without the margins or scale. Field maps are also produced with the information collected in a GPS receiver. The GPS data is downloaded into Geographic Information System program for producing digitized maps.

Field maps are used to prepare the Situation Unit map, Incident Action map, and other incident maps. It is extremely important that the information on field maps is as accurate as possible because life and death decisions are made based on this information. This section discusses how to draw a field map and use a GPS receiver for mapping.

When drawing field maps it is important to follow standards, locate your start point, and draw features and plot points following recommended procedures.

Follow Standards

Standards help ensure that maps are of consistent quality and meet the needs of those who use them.

- S.T.A.N.D.D.

  This standard helps ensure that all maps have scale, title, author, north arrow, date and time, and datum recorded either in the map legend or somewhere else on the map.

  Scale. Draw the scale at bottom of the map. If map is "not to scale" then write that on map. Map scale may change with the copying process.

  Title. Write the title at top of map. Record incident name and number as appropriate. This includes state, unit identifier, and number (example: ID-BOF-0095).

  Author. Record your name or initials in lower right corner of map.

  North arrow. Draw north arrow.

  Date. Record date and time information gathered.

  Datum. Record datum of the map used.

- Symbology Standard

    This standard helps ensure that maps are consistent and readable. Symbols must be defined in the legend.

    – Use Incident Command System (ICS) symbology, which was discussed in Chapter 1, Overview of Maps. The Fireline Handbook also has a copy of ICS symbology.

    – Additional symbols can be created as needed, but must be defined in the legend.

- Accuracy Standard

    The accuracy standard helps ensure information on the map is accurate.

    – Current and up-to-date information.

    – Features are drawn in the right location and have accurate shape and proportion.

- Utility Standard

    The utility standard helps ensure that the field maps serve the needs of the Situation Unit, Operations, Command and General Staff, and other incident personnel.

    – Complete
    – Readable
    – Submitted on time

Locate Your Start Point

Locate your start point on the map by measuring from a known point that is on the map, measuring between two points or using a GPS receiver.

Draw Features and Plot Points on Map

The features drawn on a field map will vary with each incident; however, common features include:

- Fireline
- Contingency lines
- Division breaks
- Access
- Helispots
- Hazards

- Roads and trails
- Water sources
- Spot fires
- Fuel types
- Escape routes, safety zones
- Natural barriers

- Hotspots
- Facilities/improvements
- Structures
- Potential safety zones/escape routes
- Plot points as appropriate
- Other features

Use ICS symbology to draw these features on the map and check to make sure that scale, title, author, north arrow, date and datum (S.T.A.N.D.D.) are recorded.

Use a Global Positioning System Receiver for Mapping

The data entered into a GPS receiver can be downloaded into Geographic Information System software to produce digitized maps. However, do not rely on the GPS receiver alone – always have a map and compass. Refer to the GPS receiver owner's manual for specific instructions. Some basic tips on using the GPS receiver for mapping include:

- Determine Memory Capacity of GPS Receiver

Find out what the memory capacity is for your GPS receiver. Also, determine how many track points the GPS receiver is capable of storing. If you run out of memory while you are collecting data it can result in a loss of data, decrease in accuracy of data, and other problems.

- Clear Track Log

Clear the track log before you start recording data so old data does not get mixed up with new data.

- Set the Record Mode

    - Set interval to "distance" or "time."

    The Record Mode needs to be set to a specific "distance" or "time" interval – this tells the GPS how often it should record. For example, if the record mode is set to record by distance, every

    0.01 miles, the GPS will record a track point every 53 feet. Be careful about the interval you set up because you can quickly run out of memory, for example, if the distance interval is 0.01 mile and there is 3 miles of line to track the GPS may run out of memory.

    Distance is the recommended setting. If you set it to record distance at too high of an interval, such as 0.25 miles, you may miss bends or other important features. The GPS can also be set to record at time intervals, for example every 20 seconds. However, whenever you stop, the GPS will continue to record and the points will pile up on each other.

    - Do not set the Record Mode to wrap.

    If the Record Mode is set to wrap and the GPS memory is at 100% it will start to overwrite points that were recorded at the beginning of the track. When you are ready to record and at your starting point, set the Record Mode to "Fill." If you need to back track, veer off course, take a break, etc., turn Record Mode to off. Do not turn GPS receiver unit off.

    Start a new track log for different areas, as appropriate. Setting the record mode to "Fill" tells the receiver to use the last bit of memory and then stop recording. Newer GPS receivers have the ability to convert track logs to a route. A route is permanent and will not be overwritten.

- Name and Save Track Log

    Name and save track log after recording. Keep the name short and write down the name with a description of what it is in your notes. Refer to Chapter 5, Global Positioning System, for information on how to name tracks.

- Name and Save Waypoints

    Keep notes on names and descriptions of waypoints. Refer to Chapter 5, Global Positioning System, for information on how to name waypoints.

- Check Datum

    Make sure the datum set in the GPS unit matches the datum of the map you are using.

Taking Notes

It is extremely important to take good notes when recording observations, drawing a field map, or using the GPS receiver. The notes provide further clarification of what is on the maps and other observations. Don't wait until the end of the day to write your notes because it is too hard to remember what you did. The notes should include:

- Designations/names used on the map and in the GPS receiver (examples: Access #1, A1, DP#1, DP1).

- Description of items mapped, such as capabilities and limitations of water sources.

- General observations

  - Fuel types

  - Spread rates

  - Safety/hazards

  - Fire weather

  - Distances

  - Other information, as appropriate

- Name of person who collected data and when it was collected (date and hours). Writing down the start and stop time when recording track data can help GIS personnel identify track data once it is downloaded.

- Digital photos can also accompany notes.

When writing notes, try to keep them organized and legible, not only so you can read them but others as well. There is no specific format for writing notes; however, Appendix C has a copy of a form that you can use or you can develop your own form.

Checking Your Understanding

Answers to "Checking Your Understanding" can be found in Appendix B.

1. Practice orienting a map with topographic features and with a compass.
   Refer to the map on page 141 to answer questions 2 – 6.

2. Using a protractor or compass, what is the bearing between point A and B?

3. What is the latitude/longitude coordinate of point C?

   Latitude _____   Longitude _____

1. What is the UTM coordinate of point C? The UTM zone is 11.

   Easting _____   Northing _____

2. Plot the following latitude/longitude coordinate on the map:

   Latitude 46° 53' 47" Longitude 114° 46' 33"

3. Plot the following UTM coordinate on the map:

   Zone 11 Easting 668760 Northing 5195520

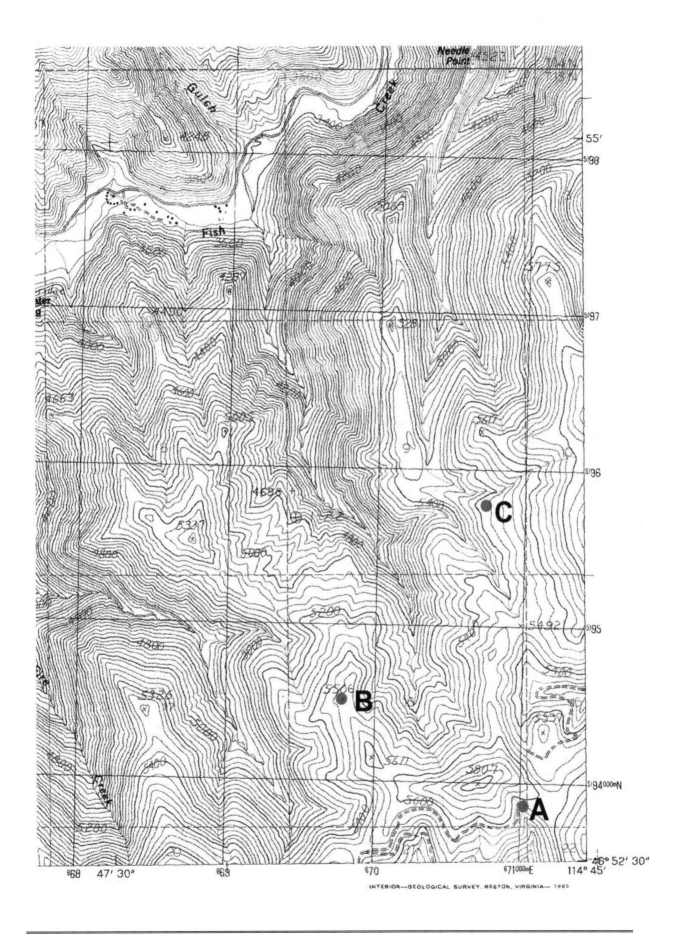

4.	When estimating your own position using triangulation, can you take bearings of a tree and large rock for drawing lines of position?

5.	You are a field observer on an incident. You see a potential hot spot several miles away and you need to radio in the location but you do not know the hot spot's location. How can you find out the location of the hot spot using a compass?

6.	Follow the directions in this chapter and determine your pace on level and sloping ground.

7.	If your average pace is 5½ feet and you walk 1700 paces on level ground, how many feet did you travel?

8.	In general, list three situations that could lengthen or shorten your pace.

9.	What are the four standards that you should incorporate when preparing field maps?

10.	Why is determining the memory capacity of your GPS receiver important?

11.	What information should be in your field notes?

APPENDIX A – GLOSSARY

Back Bearing

A back bearing is measured from the object to your position. It is the exact opposite of a direct bearing.

Base Line

An imaginary line on the ground running east-west (horizontal) measured with special accuracy to provide a base for surveying.

Cardinal Positions/Directions

North, south, east, west; used for giving directions and information from the ground or air in describing the fire (eg., the west flank or east flank, not right flank or left flank).

Compass

An instrument used for showing direction, consisting of a magnetic needle swinging freely on a pivot and pointing to magnetic north.

Contour Line

A line on a map or chart indicating elevation in feet, and connects all points of the same height above sea level.

Declination

Declination is the difference in degrees between true north and magnetic north.

Degree

A unit of angular measurement equal to one-360th part of the circumference of a circle. The entire globe contains 360 degrees, each degree contains 60 minutes, and each minute contains 60 seconds.

Graphic Scale (G.S.)

A graphic scale is a line marked off on a map which compares map distances to the ground distance in "different" units of measurements.

Landmark

A feature in the landscape which can be readily recognized; anything from a prominent tree or rock, to a church or a lake.

Latitude

Angular distance, measured in degrees, creating imaginary lines circling the earth's globe. The lines extend in an easterly and westerly direction, parallel with the equator, which is 0 degrees latitude. The degrees of latitude increase as one proceeds from the equator toward either north or south poles where the latitude is 90 degrees.

Legend

A key accompanying a map which shows information needed to interpret that map. Each type of map has information represented in a different way relating to its subject matter. The legend can explain map scales, symbols and color.

Longitude

Angular distance, measured in degrees, creating imaginary lines extending from north pole to the south pole which identify geographical positions on the earth's globe. The lines are based from the Prime Meridian of 0 degree longitude which runs through Greenwich, England, extending 180 degrees westward and eastward.

Magnetic Bearing

Bearing by magnetic north rather than true north.

Magnetic North

The direction toward which a magnetic needle of a compass points.

Map

A line drawing, to some scale, of an area of the earth's surface. It shows objects and features by conventional signs.

Map Scale

Indicates the ratio or proportion of the horizontal distance on the map to the corresponding horizontal distance on the ground.

Pace

A pace is defined as the average length of two natural steps (a count is made each time the same foot touches the ground).

Planimetric Map

A map that shows the positions of features without showing the elevations of all hills and valleys of the land. It can include rivers, lakes, roads, boundaries, or other human-made symbolic features.

Principal Meridian

An imaginary line on the ground running north-south which is accurately laid out to serve as the reference meridian in land surveys.

Representative Fraction (R.F.)

A scale that expresses the ratio of the map distance to the ground distance in 'SAME' units of measurements. It is usually written as a fraction or ratio.

Section Area

An area of land one mile square and containing 640 acres, more or less, which is one of 36 parts of a township.

Slope (percent)

The ratio between the amount of vertical rise of a slope and horizontal distance, expressed in percent. One hundred feet of rise in 100 feet of horizontal distance equals 100 percent.

Topographic Map

A map that shows the positions of features, and also represents their vertical position in a measurable form.

Topographic Terms

Depression: A low place in the ground having no outlet for surface drainage.

Hachures: A series of short, nearly parallel lines used in map making to represent a sloping surface. Representing a depression or pit, the contour line is joined forming a circle with the hachures on the inside of the circle.

Hill: A naturally occurring mass of earth material whose crest or summit is at a lower elevation than a mountain.

Mesa: A flat-topped mountain with steep sides.

Ridge:A   long narrow elevation of land; a steep slope or a similar range of hills or mountains.

Saddle: A depression or pass in a ridgeline.

Valley: A stretch of low land lying between hills or mountains which are sometimes occupied by a stream.

Township

An area of land divided by township lines and range lines which is approximately 36 miles square. Each township is divided into 36 parts, each approximately one mile square, called sections. Township lines, which are 6 miles apart, run east and west parallel to the Base Line (and also parallel to lines of latitude).

Triangulation

A method of determining the location of an unknown point by using the laws of plane trigonometry.

True Bearing

Bearing by true north rather than magnetic north.

True North

A line from any position on the earth's surface to the geographic north pole. In a declination diagram of a map true north is symbolized by a line with a star at the apex.

U.S.G.S.

United States Geological Survey of the Department of the Interior, an organization established by Congress which is engaged in topographic and geologic mapping and in collection of information about the public lands.

APPENDIX B –
CHECKING YOUR
UNDERSTANDING
ANSWERS TO EXERCISES

This page intentionally left blank.

Chapter 1

1. List three examples of how you may use a map on an incident.

    Possible answers:

    - **To assist with navigation.**

    - **To determine the location of a specific point or area (water sources, threatened resources).**

    - **To calculate distance.**

    - **To determine size of an area.**

    - **To determine terrain and vegetative cover.**

    - **To determine routes of travel.**

    - **To determine names of streets, rivers, mountains, and other features.**

    - **To visualize a specific area.**

2. Describe two key points to remember when using a map with a compass or GPS receiver.

    When using a compass with a map, an adjustment often has to be made for magnetic declination.

    When using a GPS receiver with a map, the datum for the map must be entered into the GPS receiver.

3.   Indicate the type of map that would be most appropriate for these activities:

   A.   Locate hot spots on an incident – **Infrared map**

   B.   Determine slope of a specific area – **Topographic map**

   C.   Identify travel route – **Transportation map**

   D.   Determine current perimeter location – **Situation Unit map**

   E.   Identify perimeter location when the incident started – **Progression map**

4.   What publication can you use to learn the ICS symbols?

   Wildland Fire Incident Management Field Guide – PMS210

5.   List three sources of where you can obtain maps.

   Possible sources:

   - **Federal agencies - local, regional, and national**

   - **Local/State agency offices**

   - **Local business offices**

   - **Internet**

   - **Mapping software**

Chapter 2

1. What is the fractional scale and declination of this map? If you are using a GPS receiver, what datum would you use?

    Fraction scale: **1:24,000**

    Declination: **16.5 degrees East**

    Datum: **1927 North American Datum**

2. List the reference coordinates for latitude/longitude and UTM.

    Latitude: **43° 52' 30"**

    Longitude: **115° 52' 30"**

    UTM: **^{5}91^{000m}·E. and ^{48}58^{000m}·N.**

3. Calculate the contour interval for this map.

    Step 1:   **Two index contours are 9000 feet and 9100 feet. Step 2: The difference between the two index contours: 9100 feet – 9000 feet = 100 feet.**

    Step 3:   **There are 5 lines.**

    Step 4:   **Contour interval is 20 (100 divided by 5).**

4. Draw a profile (similar to a line graph) of the land from point "a" to point "b." Elevation lines are marked in 100-foot increments. Hint: The elevation rises from the 100-foot contour line.

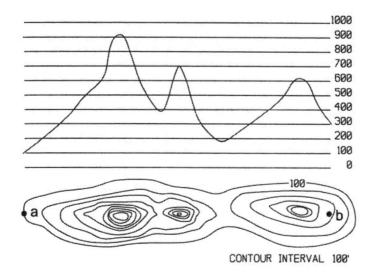

5. Identify the topographic feature inside the rectangles lettered A- F with one of these characteristics: stream, hilltop, steep terrain, ridge, depression, and flat terrain.

   A.   Hilltop
   B.   Flat terrain
   C.   Steep terrain
   D.   Ridge
   E.   Depression
   F.   Stream or drainage

6. Estimate the percent slope between A and B. What is the aspect of the slope between A and B? The scale is 1:24,000 (1 inch = 2000 feet).

   Slope: **12%**   Aspect: **SW**

   Step 1:   The elevation of point A is 9400 and point B is 9160
   Step 2:   Vertical (rise) distance is 240 feet
   Step 3:   Horizontal (run) distance is approximately 2000 feet
   Step 4:   Slope is 12% (240 ft / 2000 ft = .12)

Determine the equivalent unit of measurement for the following:

A.   **2.5 miles   = 200 chains**

B.   **1.5 chains   =   33 yards**

C.   **29,040 feet   = 5.5 miles**

D.   **3 chains x 20 chains   =   6 acres**

E.   **1/8 of a section   =   80 acres**

7. Estimate the acreage (in acres) within 10% accuracy (+ or -) of fires A- D.

A.   **80**

B.   **165**

C.   **25**

D.   **27**

This page intentionally left blank.

Chapter 3

1. What are two common global coordinate systems used in the United States?

   - **Latitude/Longitude**
   - **Universal Transverse Mercator**

2. Latitude is a measure of how far **north** or **south** a point is from the **equator.**

   Longitude is a measure of how far **east** or **west** a point is from the **prime meridian   Greenwich England.**

3. On USGS topographic maps, UTM grid lines are marked every **1000** meters.

4. This is an abbreviated UTM coordinate: ^{5}66E and ^{51}96N. How else could it be written?

   566000mE and 5196000mN

   or

   566000E and 5196000N

5. Given this UTM position in Montana – 12 683456E 5346782N – the easting is located **183,456** meters east of the 12th zone central meridian and the northing is located **5,346,782** meters north of the 12th zone equator.

6.   Write the acreage and location description (section, township and range) for each of the lettered areas.

    A.   **160**   **NW1/4, Sec. 3, T.2S., R.4E.**

    B.   **80**   **E 1/2 NE1/4, Sec.3, T2S., R.4E.**

    C.   **40**   **NW1/4 SW1/4, Sec.3, T.2S., R.4E.**

    D.   **20**   **W1/2 NW1/4 SE1/4, Sec.3, T.2S., R4E.**

    E.   **20**   **S1/2 NE1/4 SE1/4, Sec.3, T.2S., R.4E.**

    F.   **30**   **N1/2 and SW1/4 SE1/4 SW1/4, Sec.3, T.2S., R.4E**

                OR

                W1/2 and NE1/4 SE1/4 SW1/4, Sec.3, T.2S., R.4E.

    G.   **10**   **SW1/4 SE1/4 SE1/4, Sec.3, T.2S., R.4E**

    H.   **5**   **E1/2 NE1/4 SW1/4 SE1/4, Sec.3, T.2S., R.4E**

    I.   **5**   **N1/2 NW1/4 SW1/4 SE1/4, Sec.3, T.2S., R.4E**

    J.   **2 ½**   **NE1/4 SW1/4 SW1/4 SE1/4, Sec.3, T.2S., R.4E**

7.   Name two other Geographic Location Systems besides latitude/longitude, UTM, and U.S. Public Land Survey.

Possible answers:

- **Military Grid Reference System**
- **Spanish Land Grants**
- **Metes and Bounds**
- **State Land Coordinate System**

Chapter 4

1.   List three examples of how you may use a compass on an incident.

Possible answers:

- **Determine direction to a destination or landmark.**
- **Stay on a straight course to a destination or landmark, even if you lose sight of the destination or landmark.**
- **Avoid obstacles in the path to the destination or landmark.**
- **Return to your starting point.**
- **Pinpoint locations on a map and in the field.**
- **Identify what you are looking at in the field or on a map.**
- **Orient a map.**
- **Plot points on a map.**
- **Plot route of travel on a map.**

2.   Label the seven parts of a compass.

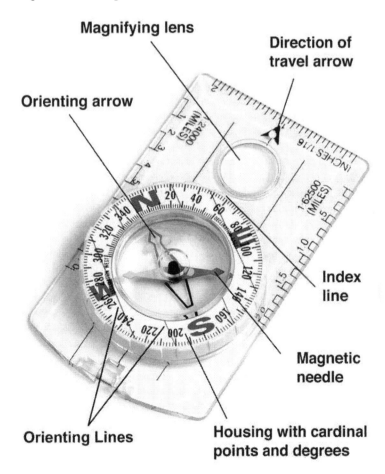

3.   List five tips on how to obtain accurate compass readings.

Possible answers:

- **Hold the compass level and steady so the needle swings freely.**

- **Hold the compass about waist high in front of the body, except when using a compass with a sighting mirror or a sighting type compass.**

- **Raise and lower eyes when taking a bearing, do not move your head. Always use the same eye when taking bearings.**

- **Directly face object that is being measured.**

- **Magnetic fields will give incorrect compass readings. Avoid taking readings near magnetic fields such as steel, iron (ferrous metals), vehicles, rebar, and clipboards. Even belt buckles and rings can interfere with the compass reading.**

- **Take bearing twice.**

- **Adjust for magnetic declination as appropriate.**

- **Follow the direction of travel arrow, not the compass needle, when walking a bearing. Always follow the line indicated by the compass rather than relying on judgment as to the direction.**

- Use back bearings to ensure you are on track when navigating.

4.   How do you adjust your compass for declination? How do you know what the declination is for the area where you are working?

- Refer to the owner's manual for instructions on adjusting a compass for declination.

- Look at the bottom left hand corner of a USGS topographic map for the magnetic declination information.

5.   What are the two different ways to orient a compass?

Orient to magnetic north or geographic north.

6.   The following exercises will improve your performance.

- Practice taking direct and back bearings of various objects.

    No answer – just practice.

- Take a compass bearing of a distant object. Mark your starting location, walk to your object. Now take a back bearing and follow that bearing. How far off were you from your starting point?

    You should be close to or at your starting point.

- Practice estimating slope using a clinometer.

    No answer – just practice.

This page intentionally left blank.

Chapter 5

1. Practice storing and naming waypoints and tracks using a GPS receiver.

   No answer – just practice.

2. Determine how many waypoints your GPS receiver can store in the memory.

   Answer will vary depending upon type of GPS receiver.

3. List three ways you can prevent making user mistakes when using a GPS receiver.

   - **Be extremely careful when entering information into the receiver.**

   - **Verify that the receiver has locked on to four satellites.**

   - **Don't hold the GPS receiver close to the body and use the antenna as appropriate. Sometimes facing the south can alleviate signal problems caused by the body.**

4. List three things that are important to do when you are taking a GPS receiver with you on an incident.

   - **Always bring a compass and map.**
   - **Have a GPS download cable.**
   - **Have extra batteries.**
   - **Know memory capacity of the GPS receiver to prevent loss of data, decrease in accuracy of data or other problems.**
   - **Bring the GPS external antennae for use while driving or flying.**
   - **Take notes that describe what you are saving in the receiver.**

5. How should you name waypoints?

   Use short descriptive names, such as D1, HL1, DP1, H1, A1.

This page intentionally left blank.

Chapter 6

1.   Practice orienting a map with topographic features and with a compass.

Keep practicing until you feel comfortable. It is much easier to practice in terrain that you are familiar with before trying to do it in unfamiliar terrain.

2.   Using a protractor or compass, what is the bearing between point A and B?

299 degrees

3.   What is the latitude/longitude coordinate of point C?

Latitude 46° 53' 45" Longitude 114° 45' 31"

4.   What is the UTM coordinate of point C? UTM zone is 11.

Zone 11 Easting 0670720 Northing 5195780

5.   Plot the following latitude/longitude coordinate on the map: Latitude 46° - 53' - 47" Longitude 114° - 46' - 33"

See map on page 166 for answer.

6.   Plot the following UTM coordinate on the map: Zone 11 Easting 668780 Northing 5195530

See map on page 166 for answer.

7.   When estimating your own position using triangulation, can you take bearings of a tree and large rock for drawing lines of position?

No, you need to use landmarks that can be found on a map.

8.   You are a field observer on an incident. You see a potential hot spot several miles away and you need to radio in the location but you do not know the hot spot's location. How can you find out the location of the hot spot using a compass?

One option is to find out if anyone else is nearby who can also see the hot spot. If so, then both of you can take a bearing and you can draw lines of intersection to determine location of the hot spot.

9.   Follow the directions in this chapter and determine your pace on level and sloping ground.

10.   If your average pace is 5½ feet and you walk 1700 paces on level ground, how many feet did you travel?

9,350 feet

11.   In general, list three situations that could lengthen or shorten your pace.

*   **Steepness of slope**
*   **Strong winds**
*   **Soft surfaces such as sand and gravel.**
*   **Wet, rainy, or icy conditions.**

12.   What are the four standards that you should incorporate when preparing field maps?

*   **S. T. A. N. D. D.**
*   **Symbology Standard**
*   **Accuracy Standard**
*   **Utility Standard**

13.   Why is determining the memory capacity of your GPS receiver important?

If you run out of memory while you are collecting data it can result in a loss of data.

14.   What information should be in your field notes?

- **Designations/names used on map and in GPS receiver (Access #1, A1, DP#1, DP1)**

- **Description of items mapped (capabilities and limitations of water sources)**

- **General observations**
  - **Fuel types**
  - **Spread rates**
  - **Safety/hazards**
  - **Fire weather**
  - **Distances**
  - **Other information, as appropriate**

- **Name of person who collected data and when it was collected (date and hours). Writing down the start and stop time when recording track data can help GIS personnel identify track data once it is downloaded.**

- **Digital photos can also accompany notes.**

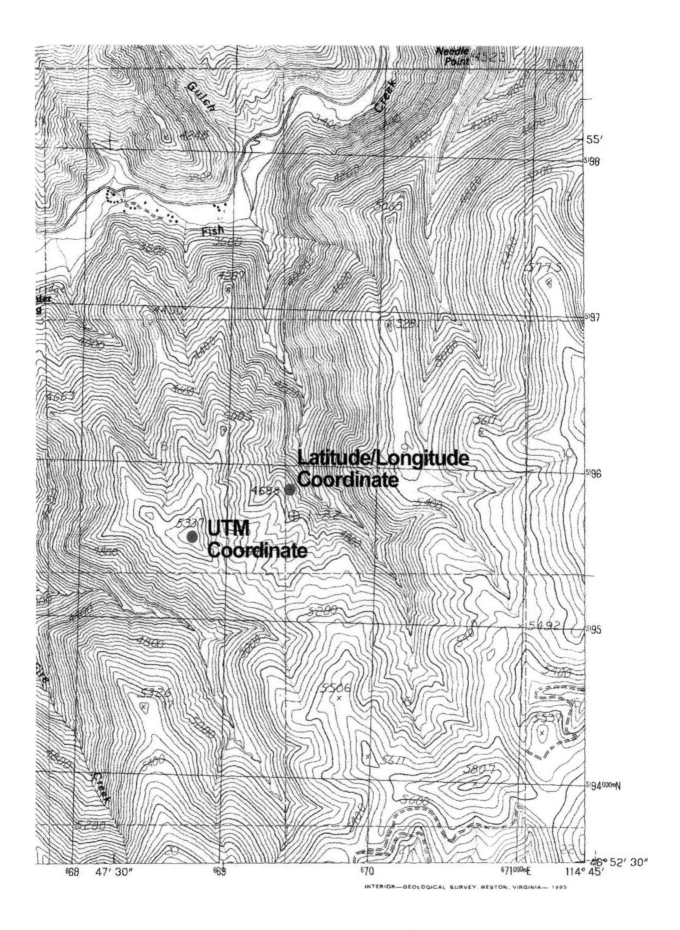

Appendix B – Basic Land Navigation

APPENDIX C –
TOOLS AND RESOURCES

This page intentionally left blank.

Appendix C – Basic Land Navigation

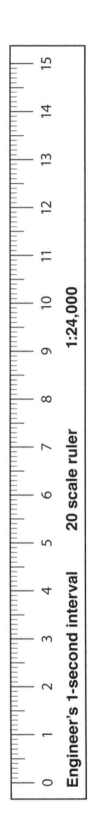

Engineer's 1-second interval   20 scale ruler

1:24,000

USGS Quadrangle Series	Map Inch Per Mile	Acres Per Square Inch	Each Dot Equals
7.5 Minute Quad	2.64	91.827	1.447 acres
15 Minute Quad	1.01	633.663	9.9101 acres

Templates – Copy on clear plastic sheets. Make sure scale does not change during photocopying.

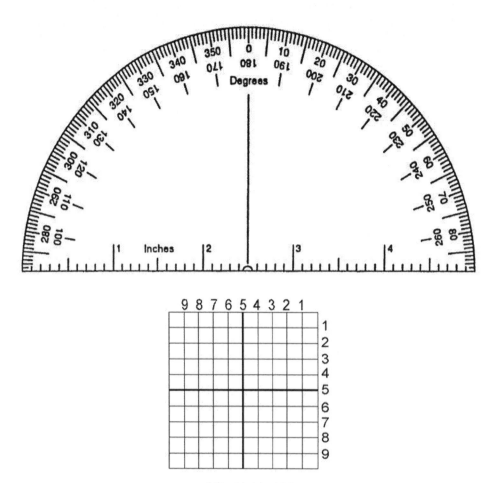

1:24,000 UTM Grid
Each mark is 100 meters

Templates – Copy on clear plastic sheets. Make sure scale does not change during photocopying.

FIELD NOTES

FIRE NAME:_____

MAP/GPS DESIGNATION	DESCRIPTION/OBSERVATIONS

DATA COLLECTED BY
(NAME/POSITION):_____

DATE:_____ AT (HRS):_____

PAGE_____ of_____

Notes:

Made in United States
Orlando, FL
27 February 2022

15177831R00096